D0438995

In God's Image After All

In God's Image After All

*How Psychology Supports
Biblical Creationism*

Paul D. Ackerman

BAKER BOOK HOUSE
Grand Rapids, Michigan 49516

Copyright © 1990 by Paul D. Ackerman
Published by Baker Books
a division of Baker Book House Company
P.O. Box 6287, Grand Rapids, MI 49516-6287

Second printing, July 1993

Printed in the United States of America

Library of Congress Cataloging-in-Publication Data

Ackerman, Paul D.
    In God's image after all: how psychology supports Biblical creation-
ism / Paul D. Ackerman.
        p. cm.
    Includes bibliographical references.
    ISBN 0-8010-0223-0
    1. Creationism. 2. Psychology, Religious. I. Title.
BS652.A25 1990
233'.11—dc20   90-41396
                                                                    CIP

Scripture quotations not otherwise identified are from the King James
Version. Other Scripture quotations are from the New American Standard
Bible (NASB) © The Lockman Foundation 1960, 1962, 1963, 1968, 1971, 1972,
1973, 1975, 1977; the New International Version (NIV) Copyright © 1973,
1978, 1984 International Bible Society, used by permission of Zondervan
Bible Publishers; and the New King James Version (NKJV) Copyright © 1979,
1980, 1982, Thomas Nelson, Inc., Publishers.

Cover and interior illustrations: Paul Stoub

To

Ellen Myers

in recognition of her pioneering work and
leadership in exploring the implications
of biblical creation for the social sciences
and humanities

Contents

Acknowledgments   9
Preface: *Knowing As We Ought*   11

1. How I Came to Write This Book   13
2. Normal Unhappiness   19
3. Puzzling Moral Inconsistencies   27
4. The Reality of Choice   39
5. Personality: *In God's Image*   47
6. Amazing Creation   55
7. Abundant Provision   63
8. Blessed Rest   75
9. We Need God   83

Appendix: *Discussion Questions*   87
Endnotes   97

Acknowledgments

I am grateful to the following friends for their help in the preparation of this book. At an early stage in manuscript development, the suggestions of Sue Paar and David Jones were very helpful. Ellen Myers, to whom this book is dedicated, has for years labored in prayer and friendly concern over this project. She was there at the beginning and at the end. Finally I wish to thank my dear friend Ed Hauser, who is a skilled artisan of the English language and helped me greatly in the polishing stage.

Preface
Knowing As We Ought

And if anyone thinks that he knows anything, he knows nothing yet as he ought to know (1 Cor. 8:2 NKJV).

One must be careful in employing scientific evidence to witness for the Bible. Science is changeable, and what we think we know today may look foolish in the light of what we think we learn tomorrow. The Christian's faith is not to stand on the shifting sands of scientific knowledge but on God and his Word. Nevertheless, Scripture itself asserts that through the creation God witnesses not only to his existence but to his "eternal power and divine nature . . . so that men are without excuse" (Rom. 1:20 NIV).[1]

One walks a fine line, in Christian humility, bearing witness to evidences supporting the truth of God's Word but stopping short of implying that the Bible is dependent on such proofs. The point is to *witness to* rather than *prove* the Bible. The goal must not be to interpret the Bible through our scientific knowledge, but to interpret and organize scientific knowledge— what we think we know—in terms of biblical revelation. The present book will seek to bear witness to biblical truth and to interpret and organize the scientific knowledge of psychology primarily around three doctrines.

First, man is created in the image of God and is not the product of evolution. Indeed, the whole universe is created and not evolved (Gen. 1, 2).

Second, due to willful disobedience of God's commandment in the Garden of Eden, man is fallen and sinful (Gen. 3). The whole of creation is subject to corruption and bondage because of Adam's and Eve's sin (Gen. 3:17; Rom. 8:19–22).

Third, man is dependent on God (Acts 17:24–28) and cannot comprehend or reason correctly independent of God; the salvation he has provided through Jesus Christ, and his revelation of earthly and heavenly truths in the Bible (John 14–16; Col. 1:15–21; Rom. 11:32–12:2).

Of course, many facets of these doctrines are spiritual and transcend the scope of what we can comprehend through scientific research. The topic of man as created in the image of God, for example, goes beyond the reach of scientific psychological research. Nevertheless, we can hope to make proper sense of the broad scope of psychology's research findings only when we consider the discipline in the light of biblical teaching about human nature. With these cautions and qualifications, we will begin our study of psychology in the context of the biblical framework. As we will see, the field provides abundant evidence echoing fundamental scriptural themes.

1

How I Came to Write This Book

Each one should remain in the situation which he was in when God called him (1 Cor. 7:20 NIV).

I was a psychologist before I became a Christian. My specialty was social psychology, and my theoretical stance was field behaviorism (which is very close to radical or Skinnerian behaviorism). During that time I was not a Christian, and I believed that Christianity was an active evil in the world. As a result of a childhood experience I believed in God, but that belief was under regular assault as I proceeded in my education and later academic life. My belief in God was vague and neither compatible nor integrated with my professional life. For one thing, regardless of whether I believed that God existed, I came in my so-called academic maturity to believe that man did not exist. In other words, I did not believe in free will.

As a behaviorist, I was what is called a "philosophical determinist." I believed that all physical, biological, and psychological events—including apparent choices and decisions—are merely the result of prior physical causes. From that viewpoint, the mental ideas and choices that seem to cause actions are themselves reflections of physical events. Of course, if I believed—in a sense—that man did not exist, then I had to believe—in that same sense—that I personally did not exist. Finally, believing—in a meaningful sense of the word—that I did not exist, I tried to teach my students that they did not exist either.

"Non-existence" was emotionally painful for me. In much of my professional and private life, I was not a happy man. As a child I had had great expectations for life. I had looked forward to it as a wonderful adventure. By thirty the expectations were gone. For one thing, as a behaviorist, I experienced people not as choosing, moral agents, but as *phenomena*. People, I thought, are "field events" like thunderstorms or the Grand Canyon. The Grand Canyon may be beautiful, but it is not "living an adventure." One does not give the Grand Canyon personal credit for its beauty. It is, or so I thought, an unintended by-product of blind, natural forces. People are the same. For example, I would not have said that a poet wrote a poem, but rather that the poem (or "poeming") happened at the particular time and space location of the poet. Before that, the poet happened as a result of a field of blind, natural forces. In my view the poet was a time-and-space field event particularly conducive to the occurrence of poems. I had learned this view from psychologist B. F. Skinner, who had applied the principles of his operant conditioning psychology to the matter of poetry.[1] To quote Skinner: "A person produces a poem and a woman produces a baby, and we call the person a poet and the woman a mother. Both are essential as loci in which vestiges of the past come together in certain combinations."[2]

Not only did I experience other people as phenomena, I experienced myself that way as well. One symptom of this was that I never saw any action or statement as original, creative, or spontaneous. All I could think of were the determining forces behind the act, idea, joke, or whatever that made it inevitable at the precise moment when it occurred. If I did forget for a moment and experienced life in the "normal" way, I was soon jolted back to the "reality" of behaviorism. Again, this view was a simple reflection of what I had learned from Skinner:

> I have been using a poem simply as an example. I could have developed the same theme in art, music, fiction, scholarship, science, invention—in short, wherever we speak of *original* behavior. . . .
>
> If I deserve any credit at all, it is simply for having served as a place in which certain processes could take place. I shall interpret your polite applause in that light.[3]

My world of "non-existence" and compartmentalized belief in God came crashing down in August of 1972 as a result of a tragic event. My five-year-old son, Bryan, was run over by a car and instantly killed. In the awful numbness of that time, something became clear. All my psychology, all the theories and theorists, were of no comfort. None of the psychologists I had studied had anything to say to me. I was still trapped in the belief that I was only a machine, but O how that machine hurt. That night, as my wife and I lay in bed, I asked her if she wanted me to pray. She said yes, so I prayed as follows: "Dear God, if it is possible, give us peace; dear God, if it is possible, bring our son back to us; and dear God, if it is possible, save our souls."

In the weeks following, things began happening to me. I became convinced anew that God was there and cared about me. I also became intensely interested in spiritual things. I had an old Bible that had been given to me as a child. I found passages where God raised children from the dead, and I placed pictures of Bryan to mark the pages. Then, during my times of private grieving, I would take out the Bible to look at my son's pictures, cry, and draw comfort from the marked verses.

I began listening to Christian radio programs and reading Christian books. Little by little I learned what Christians believed and what the Bible taught. Finally, I read a book that contained a discussion of justification by faith, as explained in the Book of Romans. The discussion struck me as being so radical that I couldn't believe it, so I turned to Romans and studied it carefully for myself. There was no doubt in my mind that the biblical Book of Romans taught exactly what the book I was reading explained about justification by faith. Though I can't tell you the hour, day, or even the month during my spiritual search following the death of my son, I did come to understand, believe, and receive the gospel of Jesus Christ. I became a Christian.

Now What?

As a new Christian, the question was what to do with psychology. First, however, I had to become familiar with the Bible. I entered a period in which I put psychology on hold and studied the Bible and basic Christian theology. The one thing I knew about psychology at this point was that if I was a Christian, I no longer was a behaviorist. Beyond that I had little to say.

It must have been in 1974 that I discovered "scientific creationism." I came across a little book by Henry Morris, the dean of modern scientific creationism. The title of the book was *The Remarkable Birth of Planet Earth*, and it contained scientific evidence and arguments for recent creation and a worldwide flood.[4] When I started to read the book I was expecting a lot of "crazy stuff." To my surprise I found that in terms of everything I had been taught about science and the use of evidence to support a point, Morris was building a sound scientific case. I could not put the book down.

As a result of reading this book, I became a convinced believer in the Genesis account of creation and early earth history as literal, historical fact. I also became fascinated with scientific creationism and the mounting evidence against Darwinian evolution. Since that time I have continued to study the creation/evolution issue, and my conviction has grown stronger that evolution is scientifically bankrupt and that the evidence supports the Bible. In 1986 I published a book aimed at explaining some of the scientific evidences for biblical creation in simple, unpretentious terms that the average person could grasp. I titled the book *It's A Young World After All*, and in its introduction I stated my view succinctly: "God is alive, the Bible is his word, and the evidence is falling into line around these two great truths."[5]

I intend this book as a sequel to the earlier one, although it deals with a very different subject matter. I centered the first book on clear and simple evidences from the natural-science disciplines of astronomy and geology; I have aimed the present book at equally clear and simple evidences from my social-science discipline, psychology. The spiritual theme of the first book was that God is near and not far off; the spiritual theme of this book is that we *need* God and cannot be our own god. I have tried to present only material that has stood the test of time and has a solid scientific, experimental basis. The issue again is biblical faith and joy in that faith. From my first encounter with creation scientists such as Henry Morris and Duane Gish and their gleaning of scientific evidences in support of the Bible from the natural sciences, I have longed that my own field might produce similar fruit. Could it be that psychology, so long a source of opposition to Christian faith, might in the end produce fruit that would draw people to God and his Word and would bless and strengthen believers? The intent of this book is to fulfill that hope.

2

Normal Unhappiness

*And he [God] said, Who told thee that thou wast
naked? Hast thou eaten of the tree, whereof I commanded thee that thou shouldest not eat? (Gen.
3:11).*

Scripture declares, and the scientific evidence from psychology echoes, that man is fallen and sinful. We disobeyed God in Eden and now bear the promised punishment for that disobedience. There is something deeply wrong with us. Even as Christians, in our fallen nature, we experience much of the weight of humankind's fallen condition.

Normal Unhappiness

Among the most common of human emotions are dissatisfaction, boredom, depression, unhappiness, bitterness, jealousy, envy, and, of course, guilt. By far the largest division of psychology is clinical psychology. This "therapy" branch of the field tries to help people alleviate the extremes of emotional distress that our fallen condition often entails. Such therapy, however, in no way claims to produce perfect emotional health and happiness but merely—when all goes well—to return a person to what one psychiatrist called "normal unhappiness." This is the condition all people experience when coping with everyday problems and stresses and trying to find something to make life endurable and meaningful.

But, in our fleshly nature, the search for meaningful life and an escape from normal unhappiness is futile. The evidence of psychology is clear. The more we have, the more we want. Today's luxury becomes tomorrow's necessity. The thing we thought would provide us escape from normal unhappiness does not. Psychologists have researched this phenomenon extensively and describe it with terms like "adaptation level" and "relative deprivation."

Adaptation Level

Remember how, as a child, you looked forward to the joy of being able to drive a car? When the time came it was wonderful, but only for a short time. By now you have adapted to the experience of driving, and it is either boring or you don't think about it at all.

We tend to take notice of things only when they depart from the usual. This is the adaptation-level mechanism. For example, when you first learned to drive, it was an unusual and pleasant experience. After you had driven for a time, it became a part of your normal experience and you stopped thinking about it. On long trips, of course, the experience becomes unusual in terms of duration and monotony, and you notice it as unpleasantly boring.

Relative Deprivation

Relative deprivation is a term that refers to our tendency to judge our lot in life not in terms of how many blessings we have but by how much we have compared to others around us. No matter how rich people are, they tend to judge their wealth by comparing themselves to others in their social group. In the West our standard of living is far beyond what most of the world's population can even conceive of; however, we do not judge our lot compared to the world standard but to that of our friends and close associates. If we do not have two cars, a color television, and a garbage disposal, we feel deprived. If we have these things, of course, they do not make us happy because of the adaptation-level phenomenon.

Illustrating this power of psychological adaptation is a study that compared reported happiness between a group of major lottery winners and a similar group of people who had not won.[1] The lottery winners had winnings ranging from fifty thousand to a million dollars, yet their reported happiness did not differ significantly from that reported by the nonwinners. On the negative side, the lottery winners actually reported taking *less* pleasure in such everyday activities as talking to a friend, watching television, eating breakfast, hearing a funny joke, getting a compliment, reading a magazine, or buying clothes. In other words, winning a huge amount of money did not make people any happier, but actually seems to have robbed them of some degree of pleasure in daily activities.

Additionally, this study examined the reported happiness of a group of accident victims who were left paraplegics or quadriplegics. Their reported present state of happiness was slightly less than that of the "normals," but their reported prospect for future happiness was as high as those of the lottery winners and the controls. The authors noted that the reported happiness of the accident victims was only slightly less than that of the others and was still on the positive end of the scale. According to the authors, the victims "did not appear nearly as unhappy as one might have expected." Psychological adaptation works to bring the experience of all people, regardless of their state of life, into the narrow, common realm of normal unhappiness.

Moral Weakness

Another facet of our fallen state is that we are *weak.* The apostle Paul expressed this fact of the human condition eloquently: "I do not understand what I do. For what I want to do I do not do, but what I hate I do" (Rom. 7:15 NIV). One of the most common New Year's resolutions is to lose weight. Two psychologists did a study of fifty-two people who had made a New Year's resolution to do so, and they carefully monitored the subjects to see how much weight they actually lost.[2] What did the psychologists find? The group as a whole achieved no significant weight loss, and some of them actually gained weight!

Weakness is a common aspect of our normal unhappiness. We don't eat as we should. We don't exercise as we should. We drink too much coffee. We smoke too much. We watch too much television. We don't read enough good literature. As Christians, we don't pray or study the Scriptures as we ought. We are not as kind as we ought to be. We gossip and complain. On and on the story goes. As Paul said, "What a wretched man I am! Who will rescue me from this body of death?" (Rom. 7:24 NIV).[3]

Sin, the Fundamental Flaw

Finally, in our fallen nature we are sinners. In our fleshly selves, we lie. We cheat. We steal. We are arrogant, proud, boastful. We constantly try to justify ourselves. We corrupt. We pollute. We destroy. We rob and kill. We will do anything for money, power, sex or success. We are also cowardly and do wrong out of timidity. The Bible declares it; our experience confirms it; daily newspapers chronicle it; and the findings of research studies in psychology add one more voice of testimony to the sad reality—we are sinners.

Laboratory Confirmation No. 1

In an experiment at Mississippi State University, students seeking to earn credit toward a course requirement arrived at the research laboratory.[4] While the subjects were waiting (in pairs) for the experiment to start, a confederate of the experimenter entered the room under the guise of looking for a lost book. In one of the experiment's conditions, the confederate struck up a conversation with the subjects and told them that he had been a previous subject in the study. The confederate then proceeded to tell the subjects several details about the experiment, along with correct answers to a multiple-choice test that would be given. (This illicit information about test answers was particularly relevant to the subjects since high scores on the test would enhance their psychology course grade.)

After the confederate left, the experimenter entered the room to begin the study. He asked the subjects if anyone had divulged information about the experiment beforehand. *Every subject lied* and told the experimenter he or she had no prior information.[5]

Laboratory Confirmation No. 2

A second example is found in one of the most famous experiments ever done in psychology. This study placed volunteer subjects in situations where an authority figure pressured them to administer what were described as excruciatingly painful and even potentially lethal electric shocks to unwilling victims.[6] Sixty-five percent of the subjects administered the potentially lethal shocks. *All the subjects* administered excruciatingly painful shocks, even when the victim protested and pleaded for release.[7]

In spite of the subjects' wrongful actions, they did not want to shock their victims. Not at all! The subjects pleaded with the authority figure to release them from his demand to shock the victim. They wanted out of the experiment. They also showed frequent signs of acute mental anguish and emotional pain. Nevertheless, they continued to give the shocks when the experimenter insisted.

Of course, the members of the research team were also guilty of harming "innocent victims." For the research personnel, the "innocent victims" were the subjects of the experiment. Yet, in spite of the mental anguish the experiment produced in these subjects, the research team continued the program through numerous replications and variations.

Participating in this multileveled victimization was one of the most prestigious American universities, which—along with its psychology department—approved of this research and allowed it to continue. "All have sinned," it is written.

Conclusion

Perhaps the easiest teaching of Scripture to demonstrate through the research evidence of psychology is that man is fallen, weak, and sinful. The scientific evidence supports the biblical description of human nature rather than the optimistic theories of the humanists. We need God and can never be our own god. In chapter 3 we will further examine evidence for not only man's fallen nature, but also his dependence on God's created reality.

3

Puzzling Moral Inconsistencies

O LORD, I know that the way of man is not in himself: It is not in man who walks to direct his own steps (Jer. 10:23 NKJV).

There is no one righteous, not even one (Rom. 3:10 NIV).

Though created in the image of God, man is still a creature dependent on his Creator and embedded in and influenced by the rest of God's creation. Besides this fundamental limitation on us as creatures, there is, apart from Christ, the weakness resulting from our fallen nature and separation from God. Man sinned and became fallen and weak. The serpent's promise that we would be like God (Gen. 3:1–5) was a lie. Rather than *being* gods ourselves, we *need* the true and living God moment by moment if we are to be saved from our sins, to transcend our inherent limitation as creatures, and to fulfill our created identities in the image of God. When informed by biblical revelation, the history of psychology becomes obvious as one more unfolding of the simple message that we are lost and need a savior.

Research on the Social Nature

In 1897, researcher N. Triplett conducted experiments that led to the discovery of a phenomenon known as "social facilitation."[1] Triplett asked subjects to do simple tasks such as winding a fishing reel as fast as possible. Subjects sometimes did the tasks with nobody watching, but at other times they had an audience observing them. What Triplett discovered—reflecting our dependence on God and his created reality—is that the audience made a difference. In every case, Triplett instructed his subjects to wind the fishing reel as fast as possible. When subjects had an audience, however, their fast-as-possible winding was faster than when they were alone. Triplett's experiments along with prodigious ensuing research showed that human actions are subject not only to the widely recognized physical and biological influences, but also to subtle social influences outside of our awareness and control.

The Search for Moral Character

In the 1920s, two psychologists, H. Hartshorne and M. A. May, began research into the nature and causes of children's moral character.[2] The idea seemed excellent. Hartshorne and May studied the moral character of eleven thousand children between the ages of eight and sixteen by exposing them to over thirty "deception tests." These tests were carefully controlled situations where children were given the opportunity, for example, to cheat on a classroom test, lie about achievement in a sporting contest, or steal a small sum of money.

In the first step of the research, Hartshorne and May hoped to identify those who had consistent moral character and, conversely, those who did not. The second step in the research would inquire into the family and educational backgrounds of the two groups of children identified in step one. Perhaps it would turn out that the children with consistent moral character all had strong Sunday school training, whereas the children lacking consistent moral character did not. At any rate, once the specifics were known, it would supposedly be easy to devise a curriculum to produce a generation of children with high moral standards and character.

What Hartshorne and May discovered was in remarkable accord with what a biblically informed psychology would expect. First, the extent of the deceit was alarming. Ninety-three percent of the children lied, cheated, or stole on at least one of the test situations. Second, there were several factors that related to deceit, and the most important of these was classroom association. "There is considerable resemblance in amount of cheating between classmates. That is, a pupil's cheating score on certain of the classroom tests is very much like that of his associates."[3]

The most perplexing finding for Hartshorne and May was the failure of honesty to emerge as a unifying personality trait.

> The results of these studies show that neither deceit nor its opposite, "honesty," are unified character traits, but rather specific functions of life situations. Most children will deceive in certain situations and not in others. Lying, cheating, and stealing as measured by the test situations used in these studies are only very loosely related. Even cheating in the classroom is rather highly specific, for a child may cheat on an arithmetic test and not on a spelling test, etc. *Whether a child will practice deceit in any given situation depends in part on his intelligence, age, home background, and the like and in part on the nature of the situation itself and his particular relation to it.*[4]

These findings support the biblical description of fallen human nature as "deceitful and desperately wicked." They also support biblical injunctions for parents to provide nurture and moral training for children. These findings, along with those from abundant later research, indicate that for moral training to be effective, parents need to be highly involved with their children and specifically address the real-life temptations that children will encounter.

Psychologists have conducted thousands of studies since the times of Triplett and Hartshorne and May. The results are consistent in showing (1) the extent to which subtle social and nonsocial features in a person's environment influence behavior, and (2) people's general lack of awareness of these influences.[5] Furthermore, as one would expect from Scripture, when confronted with evidence of these subtle influences the human tendency is to deny them and/or to steadfastly promote a self-serving, alternate rationale for one's actions.

Situational Influence vs. Moral Character

Experimental, scientific psychology provides abundant evidence that man is sinful and weak in the face of social forces and influences involving moral conduct and judgment.

1. Opinions and Attitudes

In a study at the University of Alberta, experimenters placed headphone sets on volunteer subjects and then asked them to report whether the headphones were working properly by making either vertical head movements (as in nodding your head, "yes") or horizontal head movements (as in shaking your head, "no") while listening to a radio editorial. After listening to the editorial, both groups of subjects were asked whether they agreed with the editorial. The result was that the head-nodding subjects (i.e., "yes") agreed with the editorial more than the head-shaking ("no") subjects.[6]

2. Memory and Testimony

Researchers at the University of Washington showed subjects a film of an automobile accident. One week later the experimenters asked subjects if they remembered seeing broken glass in the accident footage. The variable of concern was the effect of a changed word in one question at the time of the recall interview. The recall interrogations were identical except that for one question half of the subjects were asked: "How fast were the cars going when they *hit* each other?" The other half were asked: "How fast were the cars going when they *smashed into* each other?" When researchers asked subjects whether they remembered any broken glass, more of the "smashed into" subjects remembered broken glass than the "hit" subjects. (The accident film did not show any broken glass.)[7]

3. Impulses to Violence

A major concern of social psychologists has been to explore the causes of violence and aggression. During such research, psychologists have discovered a phenomenon dubbed as the "weapons effect," which provides a third example of human vulnerability to subtle situational influences. Male university students were given electric shocks by a fellow student and later given an opportunity to return the favor. The question was the number of shocks they would give. For some subjects, two badminton rackets were on the table near the shock key; for others, a rifle and a revolver (supposedly left from a previous experiment) were on the table. The result was that more shocks were given when the weapons were present than when the sports items were present.[8]

4. Helping Others

In somewhat more amusing research, psychologists did a fascinating study with shoppers in San Francisco and Philadelphia. The researcher posted himself near a telephone booth and waited for a shopper needing to make a phone call. While the subject (a shopper) was in the telephone booth, a confederate of the experimenter approached, carrying an armload of books. As the subject left the phone booth the confederate dropped the books nearby. The research question was whether the shopper would help the confederate pick up the books. Under normal conditions, only about 15 percent of the subjects helped, but the researchers found that by one simple manipulation they could increase the rate of helping to 85 percent. The manipulation was simply to put a dime (the price of a phone call at the time) in the return slot of the pay telephone for the subject to find when he used the phone.[9]

5. Vulnerability to Suggestion and Manipulation

Martin Orne, a well-known psychologist, sought to answer scientifically a question that is often discussed at parties and other social gatherings when the subject of hypnosis comes up. The question is: Will persons under hypnosis do things they would not do in their normal, waking state?[10] Orne thought this would be an easy research question, but he was wrong. He was never able to answer the question because he was unable to find a single thing within the bounds of professional ethics that normal, awake subjects would not do. For example, Orne would give a subject a stack of about 2,000 sheets of paper, each filled with 224 addition problems to be performed, and say, "Continue to work; I will return eventually." Orne then left the room and waited. Five and one-half hours later, with the subject still diligently working away, the experimenter gave up!

Orne then tried to revise the experiment to make the task even more frustrating. After each page of 224 addition problems was completed, subjects were instructed to tear the completed sheet into "a minimum of thirty-two pieces," get the next sheet of paper off the stack, and continue working as before. To Orne's amazement, subjects continued the work for hours with little decrement in performance and little hostility. Orne concludes:

> Thus far, we have been singularly unsuccessful in finding an experimental task which would be discontinued, or, indeed, refused by subjects in an experimental setting. . . . It became apparent that it was extremely difficult to design an experiment to test the degree of social control in hypnosis, in view of the already *very high degree of control in the experimental situation itself.*[11]

Dr. Orne dropped his quest for the answer to the hypnosis question and focused instead on the extraordinary compliance of his normal, waking subjects. He concluded that the social definition of the experimental role itself was responsible. Subjects in experiments are supposed to cooperate with the experimenter and do what they are told.

Self-Serving Bias

Hundreds of studies like those listed above indicate that we fallen creatures, far from being gods, are blown this way and that by subtle features in our surroundings of which we are not even aware. Though often unaware of what makes us do this or that, we are quick to place blame or credit for our behavior where it will do the most good in terms of our selfish interests. This tendency to attempt to justify our actions is called by psychologists "self-serving bias." People usually take credit for their successes and accomplishments, explaining them in terms of character qualities in their own personality. When it comes to sins, failures, and errors, people blame circumstances and aspects of their environment. Thus, if a person is promoted in his job, he explains the promotion in terms of his abilities, aptitudes, and other personal qualities. If he is fired, on the other hand, he blames the employer, the work environment, or the nature of the job.[12] I have been a university professor for twenty years and have learned that students take credit for their "A"s, while I get blamed for their "F"s. People who work as insurance adjusters handling accident claims continually encounter this self-serving bias.

> And how much responsibility do you suppose car drivers tend to accept for their accidents? On insurance forms, drivers have described their accidents in words such as these: "An invisible car came out of nowhere, struck my car and vanished." "As I reached an intersection, a hedge sprang up, obscuring my vision, and I did not see the other car." "A pedestrian hit me and went under my car."[13]

Spiritual Implications

What are the spiritual implications of these research findings, and how can a Christian do right in the face of powerful situational forces to the contrary? One implication appears to be that we must not place our trust in our own character and goodness. As the Bible says, "Therefore, let him who thinks he stands take heed lest he fall."(1 Cor. 10:12 NASB). But the question remains, how can Christians do the right thing as Scripture commands? Our passage goes on to provide the fundamental answer: "God is faithful, who will not allow you to be tempted beyond what you are able, *but with the temptation will provide the way of escape also, that you may be able to endure it*" (v. 13, emphasis added).

Remembering Scripture is a powerful way to escape temptation. Many times in my Christian life I have escaped a temptation as the Holy Spirit has brought to mind a relevant Scripture or biblical teaching at the proper moment. In the Gospel accounts of Peter's denial of Christ (Matt. 26:69–75; Mark 14:66–72; Luke 22:56–62), we have a good illustration. After Peter's denial, in fulfillment of Jesus' prophecy, Jesus looked at Peter, who remembered Christ's words and wept bitterly. God willing, had Peter remembered Christ's words earlier, perhaps he would not have sinned against Jesus. Remembering Christ's words when he did was apparently instrumental in Peter's repentance, forgiveness, and restoration to fellowship with God. Years ago, a Christian friend of mine gave birth to a Down's syndrome baby. She despised the baby and was tempted to suffocate it while she was nursing it in her hospital bed, planning to claim the death was an accident that occurred while she slept. As she contemplated this sinful plan, the Scripture came to her: "Inasmuch as ye have done it unto one of the least of these my brethren, ye have done it unto me" (Matt. 25:40). The baby's life was spared, and over the years she has become a wonderful blessing and companion to her mother. The point to remember is that only God is good (Luke 18:19), and we must abide in Christ through faith, prayer, and Bible reading if we are to avoid temptation and escape doing evil when temptation comes (John 15).

We can do good by incorporating biblical principles into our lives. A person can be no better than the rules or principles he or she believes in. If the principle that governs my life is "you only go around once in life, so you have to grab for all the gusto you can," then I won't do any good things that hinder my gusto grabbing. If, on the other hand, my life is based on the Christian principles of sacrifice and the Golden Rule, I will do good things for and to other people and often put their interests above my own. Bible study, proper Christian upbringing by godly parents, and Christian education are designed to instill biblical principles that serve as a basis for good conduct.

As we are informed by good rather than evil principles, we will behave better if we have hope of eternal rewards and fear of eternal judgment by God (1 John 3:3; Phil. 3:12–14; Heb. 12). Conversely, as one's faith in God, heaven, and hell are undermined, it becomes more difficult to do what is right. After my own conversion, it was the renewed faith in the existence of God, heaven, and hell that caused me to commit fully to faithfully love and cherish my wife "until death do us part." The marriages of nearly all of our non-Christian friends of that period have since broken up. If my wife and I had not become Christians, our marriage would probably also have fallen apart.

Given the fact that people are highly susceptible to tempting circumstances and situations, it is important that we associate with Christian people who share our godly values as well as our desire to live wholesome lives (Ps. 1; Prov. 1:8–19). Many Christians have stumbled in their walk with the Lord as they have become involved in questionable associations and activities.

In summary, the answer to the question of how to do right is to maintain faith in God rather than in one's self, to pray, to study the Bible, and to cultivate godly companionships.

One final note: The Bible emphasizes the need for

careful training and discipline of children.[14] In accord with biblical teaching regarding human nature and character, the best evidence from scientific psychology indicates that moral conduct is highly vulnerable to negative situations and influences. A practical implication for Christian parents and educators is that moral education of children requires much structure and monitoring. If children are to grow up *knowing* good from evil and *doing* good rather than evil, parents will have to be consistently involved in their lives. Similarly, since parents are subject to the same sin, weakness, and "situational determination" as their children, it is vital that Christians in general work to build a culture that is supportive of families and parental involvement in rearing the children. In the final analysis, since we are all weak "in our own flesh," we had better stay close to God and his Word.[15]

4

The Reality of Choice

For as the Father hath life in himself; so hath he given to the Son to have life in himself (John 5:26).

The LORD is the strength of my life (Ps. 27:1).

Studies such as those presented in the previous chapter have led psychologists to ponder the question of whether there is "anybody home" in the sense of a meaningful self that is capable of choice and of having moral character.[1] Many have concluded that there is no one home. Research has shown that experimental psychologists believe more strongly in determinism, rejecting free will and moral choice, than any other academic group.[2] By contrast, physical and biological scientists "tend toward the opposite end of the continuum. . . . Experimental psychologists . . . believe that freedom is illusory, whereas physical scientists accept freedom as a reality of life."[3] I suggest that the reason for this difference between experimental psychologists and other scientists is that experimental psychologists are continually exposed to the kinds of data presented in the previous chapter.

The rejection of free will is evidenced in amazing statements scattered through the literature of psychology:

> The truth is that you have an illusion of a psychic freedom within you which you do not want to give up.[4]

> Science . . . has simply discovered and used subtle forces which, acting upon a mechanism, give it the direction and *apparent* spontaneity which make it *seem* alive [emphasis added].[5]

> [Man] is like a molecule, randomly moving in all directions, bouncing off other particles which it encoun-

ters, and only predictable as to its direction when it is caught in a force field that keeps it on course.[6]

Scripture teaches that man is fallen and morally weak, not an "illusion," a "mechanism," or a "particle in a force field," and the evidence fits the scriptural description rather than the extremist views cited above. After the initial findings showing man's susceptibility to situational influences, more careful analysis and additional research began to uncover evidence that there was somebody home after all. For example, re-analysis of the Hartshorne and May data on moral character in school children (see chapter 3) has shown that the children did exhibit a small degree of consistency in the various deceit tests.[7] Intensive research on personality traits and attitudes has been fruitful, and psychologists are learning how to detect their influence in people's actions.

Social Engineering vs. Personality Predisposition

The influence of personality traits often becomes a problem to psychologists when they seek to develop "social engineering" programs to harness and alter the dark, *sinful* aspect of human character. Lawrence Wrightsman describes a research program carried out by Stuart Cook in which he (Cook) attempted to marshal everything psychologists have learned about social influence to assault one of the difficult problems facing societies today: racial prejudice and intolerance.[8]

Cook put together an elaborate and expensive program to change the racial attitudes of some highly prejudiced white women in a large city in the southern United States. Using previously gathered racial attitude data, Cook selected and then approached the prejudiced women to hire them for a temporary job that was to entail two hours work each day plus a one-hour, on-site lunch break. During the month of the job's duration, the white women worked in close association with a black woman who was actually the researcher's confederate. Stuart Cook applied to the job environment everything psychologists know about social influence and attitude change, as he tried to condition the prejudiced whites to be more tolerant of blacks.

Cook's black confederate was attractive, personable, capable, ambitious, and self-respecting. She was equal in job status to the white subjects, and the experimenter made sure the subjects and the black woman were treated equally and fairly. The experimenter established a cooperative reward structure for the job so that the white subjects shared both successes and failures with his black confederate. Sometimes Cook called on the white subjects to teach the black woman, while at other times he called on her to teach the whites. To provide a model for racial tolerance, the white experimenter had a black assistant to whom much responsibility was given. Finally, Cook structured the lunch breaks in such a way as to allow the black confederate to reveal positive, personal things about her life and background.

What were the results? In terms of reactions to the one black person during the time of job contact, the experience made a big difference. All the white subjects became more friendly and relaxed in the presence of the black woman during the course of that month. Some even showed a desire to continue a friendship after the job was finished. Of course, from what we already know about the impact of situations on behavior, this was expected.

In terms of general attitude change toward blacks, however, follow-up tests showed that the experimental situation had not produced a consistent effect. About 40 percent of the subjects became more tolerant in their racial views, but another 40 percent remained essentially the same in their attitudes. And 20 percent became even *more* prejudiced toward blacks as a result of the experience. Overall, there was no significant improvement.

It was obvious that factors beyond those in the elaborate, highly controlled work environment were determining the outcome. To discover what the factors were, Stuart Cook employed a fifteen-hour battery of tests to explore the personalities of his subjects. He found that those whites who did *not* change their prejudicial attitudes were distinguished by three somewhat inconsistent characteristics. They were (1) more negative in their views about people in general, (2) more tolerant of unpleasant and stressful situations, and (3) higher in self-confidence.[9] Other research supports this result in showing that the last two factors—self-confidence and tolerance of stress—are characteristics of persons generally resistant to social influence and persuasion. Such evidence shows the existence of personality and character predispositions and that humans are not mere "molecules" moving randomly in a force field.

Responsibility, Choice, and Mental Health

Belief in the reality of human choice and responsibility is important to one's mental health.[10] People who are encouraged to have a positive attitude about their ability to accomplish worthwhile and helpful objectives are healthier, happier, and more productive. Some of the best experimental evidence for the benefits of stressing personal responsibility and choices comes from research in nursing homes. In one study, for example, researchers treated elderly nursing-home patients in one of two ways.[11] For the traditional-care group, the nursing-home staff emphasized their own rather than the patients' responsibility to make the home a place the patients could be "proud of and happy in." The patients were then given three weeks of normal sympathetic care and treatment. At the end of this period, observers judged the elderly patients to have deteriorated in their general health and outlook.

By contrast, a second group of elderly patients was encouraged to take an active role in influencing policies in the home. The staff emphasized to these patients that they would have to take responsibility for their own lives and for making the home a better place to live in. The patients were then given responsibilities and decisions to make. After three weeks, the results were dramatic: 93 percent were rated as showing improved alertness, activity, and happiness.

Belief in the validity of meaningful self and consequent stressing of human choice and responsibility has been demonstrated to have benefits for both physical and mental health, personal satisfaction, and productivity. These facts are in perfect accord with the biblical record, which emphasizes throughout that God holds man responsible for his choices and gives spiritual and material rewards to those who make wise and moral choices.

In Defense of "Meaningful Self"

Students of psychology often encounter the topic of free will. As pointed out earlier, psychology is one of the most skeptical disciplines insofar as free will is concerned. One of the threats to Christian students who study psychology is that their faith comes under severe challenge when confronted with views such as those reflected by the quotes given at the beginning of this chapter. The question we turn to here is how we as Christians defend our biblical faith that man is a meaningful agent with accountability and free moral choice.[12]

Christian students must remember that the logical defense of "meaningful self," free will, or free moral choice begins with the everlasting, uncreated, all-powerful, all-knowing, *meaningful* God who has revealed his *self* in the Bible. Intellectuals who doubt free will start not with God but with primitive matter, time, and chance. These three things have no free will (meaningful self), and if our origin is strictly limited to these, we cannot logically have free will/meaningful self either. On the other hand, if we begin with God, in whose image and likeness man was created, then the defense of free will is based on the principle of Colossians 1:16–17:

> For by him [Christ] all things were created: things in heaven and on earth, visible and invisible, whether thrones or powers or rulers or authorities; all things were created by him and for him. He is before all things, and *in him all things hold together* [NIV, emphasis added].

This passage teaches that the reason every visible and invisible thing in the universe continues to exist is that Jesus Christ, who created the universe, keeps all things in existence, moment by moment. If free will is genuine and truly exists, its basis for existence is the same as everything else: the power and wisdom of Jesus Christ. The same God who creates and keeps everything else in the universe in existence must also create and keep my free will in existence.

The Bible teaches that God chooses and does whatever he wills. He created the universe not because he was compelled to or needed to but because he *chose* to do so for his own pleasure and purpose (Rev. 4:11). God has free will. The Bible also reveals that man was created in the image of God (Gen. 1:27) and therefore also exercises free moral choice and assumes accountability.

Without belief in God there is no logical basis for belief in free will. If we merely evolved by chance from unfree, lifeless, primitive matter, there would be no basis for believing that we are meaningful agents. To believe in God's existence is to believe in the possibility of your own meaningful existence; to doubt God's existence is to doubt the logical foundation for your own.

Thus we see that the foundation for our defense of meaningful self is our faith in God as creator and sustainer of the universe! We base our faith in free will on God and his Word. If we do not hold to this faith, we cannot defend free will with logical consistency. If we do hold firm in this faith, belief in free will is logical, since God has free will and the Bible teaches that we were created in God's image and likeness. Any "meaningful self" we attribute to ourselves is dependent upon God. God has life in himself (John 5:26), but we have whatever life he chooses to give and maintain in us. *We need God.*

> It is God who arms me with strength
>   and makes my way perfect.
> He makes my feet like the feet of a deer;
>   he enables me to stand on the heights.
> He trains my hands for battle;
>   my arms can bend a bow of bronze.
> You give me your shield of victory,
>   and your right hand sustains me;
>   you stoop down to make me great.
>
> Psalm 18:32–35 NIV

5

Personality
In God's Image

So God created man in his own image, in the image of God he created him; male and female he created them (Gen. 1:27 NIV).

We are fallen creatures (chapter 2), weak and susceptible to a multitude of social influences (chapter 3), and dependent upon God for our moment-by-moment existence (chapter 4). We are also created in the image and likeness of God.

Man's Creative Genius

The first and one of the most frequent things the Bible tells us about God is that he is the creator. Therefore, one aspect of our creation in God's likeness is human creativity. Consider the wonders of art and literature and the performances of great actors, dancers, and musicians. One even finds creative genius in false philosophies and religions. Through science and technology, we seem to live in a world full of miracles. Man has created space ships, airplanes, artificial hearts, polio vaccine, computers, air conditioners, and light bulbs. In my own field of psychology, we can stand in awe of the amazing creativity of psychologists in pursuit of understanding how humans think, feel, and act. The discoveries of their work testify to the creativity and genius of human beings.

To the extent that psychologists ignore or deny God as creator, they have problems with the concept of human creativity, as we saw in chapter 1 regarding B. F. Skinner's thoughts on poetry. Skinner also recognizes more clearly than most of his contemporaries the logical relation between creation by God and creativity in humans. He writes, "For the second time in a little more than a century a theory . . . is threatening a traditional belief in a creative mind. . . . Is it not rather strange that although we have abandoned that belief with respect to the creation of the world, we fight so desperately to preserve it with respect to the creation of a poem?"[1]

Skinner sees the issue clearly. If we abandon faith in the original act of creation, it is "strange" to believe in a creative mind for humans. Most psychologists, of course, find it difficult to accept the loss of the traditional concept of human creativity. Without recourse to God, however, their only resort in defending it is to lapse into what one writer called "vapory nonsense." Abraham Maslow, for example, writes: "And since self-actualization or health must ultimately be defined as the coming to pass of the fullest humanness, or as the 'Being' of the person, it is as if . . . creativity were almost synonymous with, or a sine qua non aspect of, or a defining characteristic of, essential humanness."[2]

Now, from a scientific viewpoint, what does that mean? What is "fullest humanness"? In terms of the Bible and the God of the Bible, one can understand "fullest humanness," because in Christ and in biblical revelation there is an objective frame of reference to define it. But apart from Scripture's objective—and absolute—framework, we can only have subjective opinion. Deny the Creator and you lose the meaning of human creativity either to materialist reductionism or to vapory nonsense.

Making Sense from "Confusion"

Whatever the failure of modern psychology in understanding the biblically defined foundations of human creativity, there is no repressing it in the scientific efforts of the field's many practitioners. A wonderful example is found in the work of the brilliant psychologist T. G. R. Bower. Bower's interest has focused on how newborn babies view and come to understand the world. Consider the following example of his imaginative approach to this problem.[3]

Can a baby make sense out of the world or is its

world a "buzzing confusion," as the philosopher William James thought? How do babies tell us what they see, since they cannot speak? Bower devised an ingenious way of "talking" to infants as young as six weeks of age, using a variation of the way people communicate with victims of stroke or other injury where the ability to speak and write is lost. One can work out a yes-or-no signaling system to ask the injured person questions. The communication system requires only the slightest ability for a voluntary movement. An eye blink or movement of the finger is sufficient.

Bower realized that newborn infants had a response ideally suited for establishing a "yes-or-no" communication link: head turning. A baby can turn his head as he chooses. To set up the communication link, Bower built an apparatus to play the following game with an infant. He placed a particular object in front of the baby. If the baby turned his head when the object was in place, an adult would pop up and give the baby a peek-a-boo. When the object was not in view, the baby could earn no peek-a-boo. Bower found that babies as young as two weeks of age could quickly learn to play this game, turning their heads to earn peek-a-boos only when the key object was in view.

Once the infants learned the game, the communication link was established and Bower could begin to "ask questions" to learn how infants make sense of the world. For example, he played the peek-a-boo game by using a small block positioned exactly *one* meter in front of an infant's face. Then he tested the infant by moving the block back to a distance of *three* meters. Here the question was whether an infant would respond in the same way to the block if Bower moved it from its original position. Yes, infants responded just as before, which told Bower that they "recognized" the block as the same, even though the size of the block's image on the retinas of their eyes was one-third smaller than at the time of the earlier training.

Now comes the most amazing discovery. Bower proceeded to "ask" infants questions with blocks of different sizes. For instance, what would happen if he positioned a block three times as large as the original *three* meters away from a baby instead of the *one* meter used during training? Under these conditions, the new block's retinal image would precisely match that of the original block used to train the babies.

Amazingly, Bower found that he did not fool the babies with his clever tricks. They did not respond to the new blocks, even though the size of the retinal image was the same as before. The babies' lack of head-turning responses suggested to Bower that they understood that the new block was not the same one they had seen earlier to signal that peek-a-boos were available. Research studies such as this show that babies from the first days after birth are able to interpret objects in three-dimensional space. This is called "depth perception."

Created to Understand Reality

Creative researchers such as T. G. R. Bower are making discoveries that confirm how God has designed us in such a way that we are prepared, even at birth, to make sense out of his world. A central theme of this book is that the scientific evidence from psychology supports the warning of Scripture that man cannot be his own god. If we ponder the implication of Bower's and other psychologists' discoveries about infants' innate preparation to make sense out of the world, we find another reason why this is so. The logic is simple. If we are designed to understand the world in certain pre-ordained ways from infancy, our understanding of the world is dependent on God and cannot be a matter of our own choosing. There is a reality "out there" and independent of us, but we are created to understand and fit into the framework of that reality. We can influence the reality but never make it into whatever we choose. No matter how hard we try, we cannot escape the effects of the features and characteristics that God has built into us. This is God's world, and we are part of it. We must submit to God and our created identities as creatures in his image if we want to fit into it. We can never be our own god.

The Joy of Discovery

God created us in his own image, designing us in such a way that we can understand and enjoy the miracle of his creation. Interest in scientific research and discovery is a central part of our created identity. In God's image, we long to know and understand. The foundational Scripture for this is Genesis 1:26–28, which reveals that man is created in the image of God and that God has commanded us to increase in number and to subdue and rule over the earth.[4] Another related Scripture is Proverbs 25:2: "It is the glory of God to conceal a thing: but the honour of kings is to search out a matter."

Scientific evidence in support of creativity and the joy of discovery as basic to human nature is found in the following delightful experiments with little babies.[5] As we saw above, infants can learn to turn their heads to receive a peek-a-boo from an adult. Other studies have shown that infants will learn to turn their heads to the left or the right to receive a sweet, turn on a projector to give them something to look at, or make a mobile turn. One psychologist took this research a step farther by presenting infants with puzzles to solve.[6] The researcher wired a light to a switch apparatus that an infant could activate by turning his head to the right or left. The "puzzles" were defined by the direction or combination of head turns required to make the light come on. For example, an infant might have to turn his head to the right to switch the light on. After he solved this puzzle and knew how to make the light come on whenever he wished, the rules would be changed so that only a left head-turn switched on the light. More and more complicated problems were presented until, for example, a baby might have to learn that only a combination of two right head-turns followed by two left head-turns would switch on the light.

This research revealed that infants in the first months of life are not only able to solve such puzzles, but they are intensely interested in and derive much pleasure from doing so. Once infants learn what combination of head-turns switch on a light, they show little interest in it and seldom make the head moves necessary to switch it on. It seems that the joy lies not in seeing the light but in the search for the solution to the mystery of how to control it. When the researcher changes the combination of head-turns required to switch on the light, the infants will discover this fact when they try the former solution and discover that it no longer works. When this happens, there is a sudden burst of activity by the babies until they find the new combination. At the moment of discovery—when infants learn the new solution—they *smile.* To quote from Bower:

> In the process of detecting a contingency the baby smiles vigorously. These smiles seem to be caused by discovery of the contingency and to manifest the pleasure that the baby feels at having successfully detected what to do to make a particular event happen. The smiling, in other words, indicates an intellectual pleasure, a pleasure at having discovered something about the causal structure of the world, and pleasure at being in control of some part of the world. . . . I think there is clear evidence that babies do derive great pleasure from problem solving, from intellectual mastery of some bit of their environment, from comprehension of some aspect of the causal structure of the world around them.[7]

What a joy to be that creature created in the image of God! Our dominion over the earth through science and technology and through the arts and humanities is not merely a matter of obedience to God's command in the Garden of Eden to subdue and rule over the earth (Gen. 1:28). It is a part of our created identity as well. It is also, for the believer, a part of our entering into the fullness of our Savior's joy (Matt. 25:14–23). In the next several chapters we will explore some mysteries of the human mind that God has allowed psychologists the joy of searching out.

6

Amazing Creation

*Your works are wonderful, I know that full well (Ps.
139:14 NIV).*

As Christian students look into the mysteries of mind and behavior that psychologists have long searched out, they need to keep clearly in view the biblical perspective about creation, earth history, God's existence and supernatural power, and, of course, fallen human nature. If they do so, their faith in God and his Word will be strengthened rather than shaken.

A Biblical-Creation Framework for Psychology

One of the most frequently overlooked yet vital doctrines for the Christian is biblical creation. We saw this earlier in chapter 4 on defending "meaningful self" and free will. As another example of its importance, we will consider the topic of human development.

On the basis of biblical creation, we insist that—contrary to the evolutionist dogma of our day—inferior-to-superior self-generation is impossible. A sound, biblically informed science affirms that superior forms give rise to inferior forms, with the exception and absolute upper limit being reproduction, where a highly complex living thing replicates itself and thereby creates a second, equally complex form.

Scripture begins with God, who is infinitely superior to his creation. The first man, Adam, in his original created state, is vastly superior to what he was after the fall. Man, of course, "creates" and "invents" and thereby transforms the inferior to the superior, but the greatest of our technological achievements—computers, space ships, or whatever—are nevertheless miniscule compared to the sophistication of the human minds and bodies that create them.

In the field of biology, discoveries of the cell's DNA code and later advances in molecular biology have revolutionized our understanding of physiological development. Our newly gained appreciation of the cell's bewildering complexity allows us for the first time to have a glimmer of how the cell is able to produce an adult specimen. Once thought to be an "empty room" or "undifferentiated mass," the modern view of the cell is more like a futuristic, high-technology factory. Michael Denton elaborates:

> To grasp the reality of life as it has been revealed by molecular biology, we must magnify a cell a thousand million times until it . . . resembles a giant airship large enough to cover a great city like London or New York. What we would then see would be an object of unparalleled complexity and adaptive design. On the surface of the cell we would see millions of openings, like the port holes of a vast space ship, opening and closing to allow a continual stream of materials to flow in and out. If we were to enter one of these openings we would find ourselves in a world of supreme technology and bewildering complexity. We would see endless highly organized corridors and conduits branching in every direction away from the perimeter of the cell, some leading to the central memory bank . . . and others to assembly plants and processing units. . . . A huge range of products and raw materials would shuttle along all the manifold conduits in a highly ordered fashion to and from all the various assembly plants in the outer regions of the cell.
>
> We would wonder at the level of control implicit in the movement of so many objects down so many seemingly endless conduits, all in perfect unison. We would see all around us, in every direction we looked, all sorts of robot-like machines. We would notice that the simplest of the functional components of the cell . . . were astonishingly, complex pieces of molecular machinery. . . . We would wonder even more as we watched the strangely purposeful activities of these weird molecular machines. . . .
>
> What we would be witnessing would be an object resembling an immense automated factory, a factory larger than a city and carrying out almost as many

unique functions as all the manufacturing activities of man on earth. However, it would be a factory which would have one capacity not equaled in any of our own most advanced machines, for it would be capable of replicating its entire structure within a matter of a few hours. To witness such an act at a magnification of one thousand million times would be an awe-inspiring spectacle.[1]

In psychology we lag far behind biology. Current theoretical views of the mind of the newborn are still wedded to the evolutionist, inferior-to-superior notion. Thus, the mind of the infant is viewed as either nonexistent (the "blank slate" imagined by John Locke and the modern behaviorists) or primitive and informationally inferior to the adult mind it will become (the "sensory-motor" intelligence of the cognitive psychologists).

From the standpoint of a biblically informed and scientifically sound psychology, however, such theories must fall short. When we look at a fertilized, reproductive cell, we are looking at an incredibly complex "factory" that is *well able* to create an adult of its own kind. Similarly, when we hold a newborn baby in our arms, we must surely be looking into the eyes of an intelligence that contains some psychological counterpart of the biological DNA code and is *well able* to create the adult human mind, including its intelligence, wisdom, and understanding.

"Fearfully and Wonderfully Made": Designed for Contingency

As with the biological cell, we affirm that all of God's creation is wonderfully made and *well able* to accomplish its divinely ordained purpose. Following this biblically based line of reasoning, we can begin to understand some of the remarkable things psychologists are discovering about human development and learning. Let me explain.

In studying development, psychologists focus on two broad categories of influence: (1) biological and genetic endowment, and (2) education and environmental experience. As this research has progressed, a remarkable feature of psychological functioning has become apparent. If we consider an example of one of the most wonderful and "intelligent" creations of human hands, we can begin to appreciate what scientists are discovering about ourselves as intelligently created beings.

A few years ago, United States NASA space scientists designed and built two "fearful and wonderful" spacecraft to land on and explore the surface of the planet Mars.[2] On reaching the planet's surface an interesting thing happened to one of the landers. An electrical switch malfunctioned, and an important mechanical arm designed to sample the Martian soil would not move. The project scientists, however, did not throw up their hands in despair. Instead, they began studying the electrical circuit diagrams of the spacecraft and after a time succeeded in bypassing the faulty switch, allowing the arm to work and complete its research mission.

Now one might wonder how this switch-bypassing across millions of miles of space was possible. If a house light switch is faulty, it must be manually replaced. One could not bypass it from the next room, let alone from another world millions of miles away.

The answer is simple. The NASA scientists were able to bypass the faulty electrical switch across millions of miles of space because highly intelligent and well-trained engineers designed the spacecraft in anticipation of this and many other possible mechanical, electrical, or computer failures. When the scientists discovered the failure, they were able to communicate to the spacecraft's on-board computers via radio signals from earth. Through this communication they were able to determine the location of the malfunction and send instructions back to the Mars lander's computers on how to bypass the breakdown. The scientists were able to do all this because, when they designed and built the spacecraft back on earth, they specifically constructed it to allow for such remote-control repairs. In other words, the spacecraft repair was the result of advanced planning and intelligent design.

The Mars lander was not merely designed to operate on the surface of Mars. It was also designed to take into account a wide range of conceivable, alternative modes of operation, should mechanical damage or failure occur. The craft was in effect "over-designed," or *designed for contingency*. Psychologists and biologists have discovered remarkable evidence that confirms what we would expect, based on the biblical account of creation. Humans, and all living creatures, show many examples of contingency- or over-design.[3]

Among the most obvious examples of contingency-design are the many instances of dual organs. We have two eyes, ears, lungs, and kidneys. Without suggesting that dual organs represent mere duplication, the fact remains that a person is able to survive very well with just one. Scientists have discovered the same phenomenon in the domain of psychology. Concerning perception, for example, psychologists have determined that perceptual object and depth processing in infants is equally good regardless of whether they use both eyes or have one covered by a blindfold.[4] In other words, although some of the richness of the experience of depth perception is lost, humans and many animals have been built in such a way that they can function well even with the loss of one eye.

Another example of contingency-design is the amazing degree of adaptability to changing environments exhibited by creatures. This is true at both the species and individual levels. Scientists call the domain of scientific research related to this discovery *microevolution,* which simply means small adaptive changes by creatures and species that enable them to survive disruptions and changes in their habitats. We should not confuse microevolution with either *macroevolution,* which suggests that all living forms developed from a common ancestor, or the *general theory of evolution,* which suggests that the entire universe spontaneously arose from an homogeneous mass that exploded twenty billion years ago.[5] The scientific evidence clearly proves that there are firm limits or boundaries to the amount of adaptation of living things to environmental changes— as expected, based on God's "after their kind" creation (Gen. 1:11, 12, 21, 24, 25). Within the ordained limits, however, God has designed his creatures with abundant flexibility and provision for coping and adaptation. The facts as we know them mirror the biblical truth that God is a God of law and righteousness who must be obeyed—and also that he is a God who loves and abundantly provides for his creatures.

7

Abundant Provision

My cup runneth over (Ps. 23:5).
*I can do all things through Christ who strengthens
me (Phil. 4:13 NKJV).*

In the science of psychology, contingency-design is most interestingly exhibited in the relationship between biological preparedness and instinctual programming on the one hand and learning and adaptive capability on the other. In a sense, we are similar to airplanes that are designed with both computerized, automatic pilots and manual controls. A person can either switch on the automatic pilot and rest while the airplane flies itself or assume manual control and do intricate and specialized maneuvers.[1]

In this analogy, the automatic pilot stands for the genetic programs and biological machinery that help develop and maintain normal psychological functioning. The manual controls, on the other hand, stand for the flexibility and learning capacity exhibited by humans that enable them not only to adapt to highly unusual environments but, as we shall see, to provide backup when the genetic biological programming is damaged. Similarly, if the learning environment is less than optimal, a person is still able to develop adequately because of his or her inherent biological programming. In other words, the instinctual and learning capacities of creatures are not merely complementary. They exhibit overlap and thus contingency- or over-design.

Biological Preparation

Genetic Programming for Social Responsiveness

Evidence that biological programming contributes to abilities generally considered to stem only from learning and education has been surfacing over the years. Much of this evidence comes from research with animals.

For example, a research study by G. P. Sackett kept infant monkeys in isolation from birth and at various times exposed them to photographs of other monkeys.[2] Some pictures depicted adult male monkeys in threatening postures. Shortly after birth the baby (subject) monkeys began to respond to the threatening photographs. At first they showed exploratory and playful interest in these particular photographs. As the days passed, however, the baby monkeys began to show signs of fear and disturbance in the presence of, and *only* in the presence of, the threatening pictures. No fear was shown in response to any other types of monkey photographs. The amazing thing about this finding is that the baby monkeys showed signs of developing an appropriate fear of angry males even though they had never experienced a negative or painful encounter with them.

As further support for this interpretation, Sackett found that if the infant monkeys were given control over the presentation of various categories of photographs by a response lever, they would press the lever repeatedly to view pictures of other infant monkeys, but after a time avoided levers that produced the threatening photographs. If such social instincts are present in animals, it is possible that God has designed them into people as well.

Investigators have found direct evidence for social instincts in humans in several areas. For instance, psychologists have discovered that infants as young as twelve days are able to imitate certain facial expressions (stick out the tongue, for example) and manual gestures (wiggling the fingers) presented to them by an adult.[3] To appreciate how miraculous this is, stop to consider what a baby must do to imitate a facial expression. To imitate a spoken word is not so remarkable, perhaps, because the sound of the word as it strikes the baby's ear is structurally the same regardless of whether the baby speaks or someone else does. If a baby makes a sound that imitates another sound he or she is hearing, it would be recognizable as a match.

In imitating facial expressions, on the other hand, we have a task that is vastly more complicated, since there is no relation between the sight of a face with the tongue sticking out and the way a baby's face feels as he or she sticks out the tongue. Keep in mind that a baby in the first months of life has had no experience looking at his or her image in a mirror to learn how different facial expressions feel. Therefore, it is reasonable to conclude that genetic programming is responsible and that God has designed infants with the capability of equating their own unseen behaviors with gestures and expressions they see others make.

Language Acquisition

Another example of biological design for psychological growth and development is in the area of language acquisition. Current evidence points to much specific biological programming that enables a baby to discover and construct his or her language rather than merely learn it from scratch. This designed preparedness is evident from birth as newborn babies exhibit particular responsiveness to human speech. Scientists have discovered that babies are particularly attentive to the frequency range of the human voice and the sound patterns of speech.[4] Newborn infants are adept at making distinctions between speech sounds found in all the world's languages. By three days of age, they prefer their own mother's voice and will suck a nipple to hear it. Human speech in general is more rewarding to infants than other sounds.

Babies also show evidence of preparation for human conversation. Newborns can initiate interactions by making eye contact and terminate them by looking away. By three months, a baby can engage in "conversational turn-taking" by exchanging vocalizations with an adult. The baby vocalizes, waits for a reply, and then vocalizes again. By four months, infants can track an adult's visual regard so as to look at the same thing the adult sees. This skill is very helpful to learning word labels for things.[5]

The evidence that humans have been created with sophisticated biological programming for acquiring language continues as the child grows to adulthood. When exposed to normal social interaction, children seem to grow automatically into their language ability. With minimal training and apparently haphazard learning conditions, they are able to master their native language with remarkable ease and regularity. A leading researcher in this area is Noam Chomsky, who describes the process as follows:

> The child discovers the theory of his language with only small amounts of data from that language. . . . His theory of the language . . . enables the child to reject a great deal of the very data on which the theory has been constructed. Normal speech consists, in large part, of fragments, false starts, blends, and other distortions of the underlying idealized forms. This is a remarkable fact. We must also bear in mind that the child constructs this ideal theory without explicit instruction . . . and that this achievement is relatively independent of intelligence or the particular course of experience.[6]

Chomsky goes on to conclude that the basis for this development is genetic biological programming. "What evidence is now available supports the view that all human languages share deep-seated properties of organization and structure. These properties . . . can be assumed to be an innate mental endowment."[7]

For the Christian, this finding is fully expected since, according to Scripture, language is part of our created identity in the image of God, the Word. Adam spoke from the moment of his creation and on the first day of his life named all the animals (Gen. 2:19). For the evolutionist, on the other hand, language origin presents a nasty problem. As a committed evolutionist, Chomsky, for example, finds the results of his research on language acquisition in children puzzling. He asks,

> How does the human mind come to have the innate properties that underlie acquisition of knowledge? . . . The process by which the human mind has achieved its present state of complexity and its particular form of innate organization are a complete mystery. . . . It is perfectly safe to attribute this to evolution, so long as we bear in mind that there is no substance to this assertion—it amounts to nothing more than the belief that there is surely some naturalistic explanation for these phenomena.[8]

Evolutionist theories of language origin start with the grunts, squeaks, and howls of simple animal communication. Some evolutionists speculate that after humans discovered fire and therefore sat around looking at each other face to face each night with nothing else to do, the primitive communication system of grunts and gestures evolved upward to the complex language of the present day.[9] But, as Henry Morris has pointed out, such speculation is contrary to the scientific and historical evidence.[10] Observations of animal communication reveal no spontaneous tendency to evolve upward; the earliest known languages and languages of so-called primitive people today are, if anything, more complex than their modern or civilized human counterparts;[11] and studies of languages over time reveal that they tend to simplify rather than become more complex. In the words of one expert, "The evolution of language, at least within the historical period, is a story of progressive *simplification.*"[12] In so many areas of psychology research, we find clear evidence that man is fearfully and wonderfully made, and that God provides abundantly for us and, of course, for all his creatures.

Learning and Adaptation

Just as we exhibit amazing evidences of biological programming and preparation for life as creatures in the image of God, so also do we exhibit remarkable adaptability and flexibility. We can learn to accomplish incredible feats. Furthermore, this ability to learn and adapt does not merely complement our biological programming. It provides genuine back-up capability.

Evidence of contingency-design is often most dramatic in cases involving severe physiological injury or disease. Such a case received national attention a few years ago in a report by Ronald Kotulak of the *Chicago Tribune*.[13] To save a youngster's life from the effects of a severe brain disease, surgeons removed the entire left half, or "hemisphere," of his brain.

Believing that the crucial brain centers for speech and language are located in the left hemisphere, the boy's doctors predicted that he would never be able to speak or use language in a normal manner. As often occurs, however, the experts were mistaken. "Ever since the operation [the young man] has been dumbfounding the medical profession. Doctors who examine him shake their heads in disbelief."[14] By the age of nine, the boy's intellectual capacity was measured in the dull-normal range. By the age of twenty-one, his verbal IQ scores had risen to the bright-normal range. Finally, tests at age twenty-six showed him to be scoring in the superior range for verbal intelligence. "Everything science knows about the brain says it's impossible for [this young man] to be doing as well as he is. Pages of medical textbooks will have to be ripped out and rewritten."[15]

"Is Your Brain Really Necessary?"

A report in *Science* carried the provocative title, "Is Your Brain Really Necessary?"[16] The article reports on the research of John Lorber, a British neurologist, who has made some remarkable discoveries about people who suffer from hydrocephalus, "water on the brain." Quoting from the report:

> Lorber was not jesting totally when he addressed a conference of pediatricians with a paper entitled "Is your brain really necessary?" Lorber believes that his

observations on a series of hydrocephalics who have severely reduced brain tissue throws into question many traditional notions about the brain. . . .

"There's a young student at this university," says Lorber, "who has an IQ of 126, has gained a first-class honors degree in mathematics, and is socially completely normal. And yet the boy has virtually no brain."[17]

A physician noticed that the student's head was slightly larger than normal and, knowing of Lorber's research interest, referred the student to Lorber for study. When Lorber did a brain scan on the boy he found to his amazement that the cranium was filled mainly with cerebrospinal fluid. "Instead of the normal 4.5-centimeter thickness of brain tissue between the ventricles and the cortical surface, there was just a thin layer . . . measuring a millimeter or so."[18] The report continues by pointing out that as startling as this case is, it is nothing new to the medical world. Many similar accounts have appeared in the medical literature over the years.

Based on his research, Lorber divides hydrocephalus sufferers into four categories based on the amount of fluid present in the patient's cranium. In the most severe category, 95 percent of the cranium is filled with fluid. Many people in this group are severely disabled, but Lorber has found that most of them have normal intellectual and social functioning: "Half of them have IQ's greater than 100."[19] The report concludes by pointing out that "although Lorber's work doesn't demonstrate that we don't need a brain, it does show that the brain can work in conditions we would have thought impossible."[20]

Hope for the Retarded

Another dramatic evidence of contingency-design that is coming to light is the capability of people suffering with various forms of mental retardation to learn and achieve productive lives. Until recently, experts in most areas of medicine and psychology were ignorant of the capability of humans and other created organisms to bypass and compensate for physical abnormalities and injuries that affected the brain. As a result, physicians and counselors have burdened parents of mentally handicapped children for decades with overly pessimistic counsel. One close friend with a Down's syndrome child was told that "fortunately they do not live very long." This remark was intended to be comforting. Far too often, parents of handicapped children have been wrongly counseled by "experts" that the child would be better off if placed in an institution.

Much of what we have been discovering about God's contingency-design of his creatures has come from parents and afflicted persons who refused to believe the counsel given them by experts. You might say that in this area the "experts" have been slowly catching up with the non-experts.

A famous case in point is that of a Down's syndrome child named Nigel Hunt. When Nigel was only two weeks old his parents were told *by experts* that no matter how much love and care they gave him, he would always be an idiot. Nothing they could do would alter the fact, they were told. Fortunately for Nigel, his parents refused to believe this negative prognosis. With great patience Nigel's mother worked with him. Making a game out of her lessons, she began to spell out words phonically as soon as Nigel could talk. Nigel rewarded his mother's devotion, for by the time he started school he could read better than most of the children in his class.

As Nigel grew older his accomplishments continued. He taught himself to type, using his father's typewriter. Then, at age seventeen, he became the first Down's syndrome individual ever to write a book. It was Nigel Hunt's autobiography, and later, with the help of his father, who wrote an introduction explaining the background of Nigel's life, the book was published under the title *The World of Nigel Hunt*.[21]

In the years since the story of Nigel Hunt became known, tremendous advances have occurred in our knowledge about education for the mentally handicapped. Once considered beyond education, it is now commonplace for Down's syndrome and other mentally handicapped children to learn reading, writing, and basic math skills. Just as with the rest of us, they require love, patience, and opportunities to learn; but, if parents and teachers provide these needs, handicapped children are well able to achieve fulfilling lives that bring joy to their families and communities. I believe that one of the implications of a biblical approach to psychology is that people we call "mentally handicapped" might more reasonably be viewed as gifted for special kinds of service. I believe that with proper training, retarded people would make excellent teachers and caretakers for preschool and early primary grade children. They would be much more patient with the slow mental pace of little children learning basic academic skills, and they might even be more perceptive about how little ones think and thus better able to explain things to them. There is one documented study in the research literature where retarded persons proved to be marvelous therapists in restoring thirteen emotionally deprived and abused children, who were severely mentally retarded as a result, to completely normal intellectual and social functioning.[22] In chapter 3 I wrote of a friend who had a child with Down's syndrome. The child's name is Becky, and she is now a young woman. Some months back, Becky, her mother, and I were driving to a local restaurant for lunch. As we turned the corner and the restaurant came into view, Becky said, "Life is good." Indeed, in Christ, it is.

A Reason to Search

Contingency-design represents more than a scientific discovery consistent with the biblical view. Confidence in contingency-design is an important and practical part of our faith in the kindness, mercy, and provision of our heavenly Father. If there is a problem, there must be a solution. If there is a disease, there must be a cure. If there is a thirst, there must be a water that quenches the thirst. Because of our faith in God, including our faith in his wisdom as the creator of the world, we persevere and endure. We continue in hope against all odds and in the face of all adversity. In the domain of science, we continue to research and study. There must be an answer; there must be a solution. No matter how intractable the mystery, the scientist continues the quest because he or she holds fast to the faith: "It is the glory of God to conceal a matter; to search out a matter is the glory of kings." (Prov. 25:2 NIV). In the next chapter we will examine some of the deeper mysteries that psychologists have "searched out."

8

Blessed Rest

*He himself gives all men life and breath and every-
thing else. . . . For in him we live and move and have
our being (Acts 17:25, 28 NIV).*

We began this book by facing the evidence corresponding to the scriptural revelation that man is sinful, fallen, and weak. Then we looked at the positive side of man's creative genius, joy of discovery, and ability to cope and master the challenges of everyday life. Now we are going to probe deeper and explore a world that is hidden from our awareness. We will discover a secret domain reflecting God's moment-by-moment provision for our lives.

"In him we live and move and have our being." Underneath the conscious arena of thoughts, feelings, choices, and actions, psychologists have explored the mysterious and hidden realm of mechanism, system, and substance on which our being rests. Through this underlying realm, God establishes limits and provides coherence and predictability to our existence. Through this realm, he also provides rest and security in the sense that myriads of essential needs are met without thought or effort on our part.

Conditioning: "Automatic Learning"

I once heard of a person with a diseased condition that entailed the loss of the ability for automatic, involuntary breathing. The individual had to take every breath consciously. What a curse such a disease would be, and what a marvelous blessing the gift of automatic breathing is. In the psychological realm, scientists have discovered similar blessed mechanisms. Among the more exhaustively researched are unconscious learning mechanisms encompassed by the term *conditioning*.

Conditioning refers to the orchestrated relationship that automatically and unconsciously develops between a living organism's responses and the environmental

76

events that for some reason or other are contingent upon them. For example, a person's subtle manner and pattern of responses in working with a machine adapt to the details of that particular machine's operation. As the machine gets older and develops minor idiosyncrasies, we easily adapt and harmonize our actions with them.[1] We are comfortable with the machine we are used to, and it works well for us.

One of the positive implications of conditioning, or "automatic learning," from a biblical point of view is *rest,* in the sense that in everyday life we find ourselves effortlessly and unconsciously adapting to environmental contingencies and maximizing favorable outcomes and events.

For example, several years ago I was teaching a large lecture class in psychology. As part of the course requirements, students had to complete a rule-enforcement or discipline project. A few students were at a loss about what to do until they hit upon the idea of using me as the object of their study. They had noted that as I lectured I often wandered around the front of the classroom from the left to the right of the lectern. Further observation revealed that about 80 percent of my lecture time was spent on the right side of the room. Without telling me, the students began a program to change my habit of preferring the right side.

The conspirators determined that on those infrequent occasions when I came to the left side of the lectern, they would reward me with quietness and rapt attention. When I ventured to my customary right side, however, they gave me inattention, paper shuffling, pencil tapping, coughing, and fidgeting. Within three days I mastered the new contingencies without the slightest awareness of what was happening. I now spent virtually all my time on the left side of the room, and, on those occasions when I paced toward the right, I would immediately turn back to the left when the tapping and coughing began.

The point I emphasize is that my adaptation to the students' "rule" was unconscious and automatic. It would be as accurate to say that I controlled the students as to say the students controlled me. They controlled me by a conscious and deliberate plan of action. I, in turn, controlled them, not by deliberate plan and choice, but by the automatic conditioning mechanism designed into my biological machinery. During the time of the students' venture, my thoughts and energies were focused on the content of the subject matter I was teaching.

Conditioned responses are among the most blessed of God's provisions for us. I can thereby drive around the city where I live, visiting freely and attentively with a friend in the seat beside me. Without effort I automatically obey traffic rules, stop at appropriate lights and signs, and (Lord willing) arrive safely at my destination. It is a sometimes frightening experience to have driven across town and upon arriving safely at home realize that I can scarcely remember the trip because of thinking about some business of the day. A good part of this ability develops because of the conditioning mechanism.

A moment's reflection will make it apparent that it is dangerous folly to do anything that would weaken the automatic habits that allow us to obey traffic and safety regulations unconsciously. This is one important reason we should consistently obey such traffic laws as coming to a full stop at stop signs and looking both ways before proceeding, regardless of time of day or amount of traffic present.[2]

Conditioning mechanisms provide rest from conscious attention to every minute detail of life. In every aspect of psychological functioning there are similar mechanisms that psychologists have discovered and explored. Much of human remembering and problem solving operate unconsciously and automatically without effort on our part.

Perception

We find another example of unconscious psychological mechanisms that provide structure and coherence to our existence in a set of phenomena known to psychologists as "perceptual constancies." To help understand these mechanisms and appreciate the important role they play in our lives, we will focus on one of the most widely researched and understood: size constancy.

When I stand in my classroom to teach my university courses, I look out on a large auditorium filled with students. Some students sit in the front row and thus are very close to me. Others in the back rows are far away. Yet, as I look at them, they all appear to be normal-size people. It is all so commonplace that I don't realize something odd is happening to me. A marvelous thing is going on as I view the class, but it is hidden from me by a "veil of obviousness" as my old professor, the great psychologist Fritz Heider, used to say.

To appreciate the mystery, I need only to hold a ruler up to my line of vision to mark the actual size of the image coming from the persons in the back row as opposed to those in the front row. The image from the people in the front row is several times larger than the image from people in the back row. Yet I am *perceptually* unaware of this fact. Psychologists call this phenomenon "size constancy," and what it means is that we tend to see familiar objects according to their actual size regardless of their distance from us.

"So what!" you say. Maybe I can give a simple exercise to help you appreciate constancies a little more. Close your left eye and place your right index finger against your face next to your right eye. Now, gently move your open, right eye by pressing your finger repeatedly against the eyelid. As you do, you will notice that the scene in front of you appears to move.

For the second part of the experiment, stand up and make fast little jumps with your whole body. Notice that unlike your earlier experience when you moved your eye with your finger, the scene does not jump around but appears fixed in front of you. It is as though your body knows that it is you and not the world that is moving, and so your perception compensates for the body's movements and provides you with a stable percept. When you remain still, however, and move your eye with your finger, your body is not able to take this into account, and so the constancy related to perceiving the surrounding environment does not function and the scene dizzily jumps before your eyes.

Glasses That Turn the World Upside Down

Psychologists have done research in which volunteers wore specially prepared glasses that distort the visual field in certain ways. Scientists use such studies to understand more about how our perception works and develops. In some studies, the distorting glasses invert the visual field so that the world appears upside down. A fascinating thing happens when subjects first put on the inverting-lens glasses. Among the disorienting effects is a loss of the constancy that produces visual-field stability. When the subject moves his head, objects appear to move and swing in front of him. After a short time the visual mechanism adapts to the distortion and visual-field stability is reestablished. If the subject continues to wear only the inverted lenses for several weeks, then, when the lenses are finally removed so the subject can return to normal vision, the stability constancy has once again been lost, and for a short period objects appear to swing around when the head is moved.[3]

Object Permanence

Another essential constancy for our lives is called "object permanence" or sometimes "object constancy." Object permanence is another important, automatic process that we do not appreciate. It refers to our awareness that things continue to exist even when we cannot see them. In practical terms, it is the ability to remember and think about absent objects. Without object permanence, life as we know it would not be possible. For example, if I drove my car to the grocery store and left it in the parking lot, I would not only be unable to find my car again, but I could not even remember that I had one to begin with. Of course, the example is ridiculous, because without object permanence I could not remember the grocery store or how to get there.

In the first days of life after birth, babies show that in a rudimentary sense they have object permanence. For example, as we saw in chapter 7, babies not yet a month old can imitate facial expressions such as sticking out the tongue, even when there is a momentary delay between viewing the facial expression and being free to imitate it.[4]

But then, mysteriously, object permanence seems to disappear in some ways. Babies go through a period in the first year of life when in certain situations they act as though they did not have object permanence.[5] It is at this age that the phrase "like taking candy from a baby" has its significance.

If you have a baby about six to seven months old, you can try an experiment and perhaps observe a milestone in his or her development of object permanence. Sit on the floor with your baby facing you. Between you and your baby there should be a small pillow. Now, hold up a small trinket or toy. The baby will, of course, want to grab it. Before he or she can do so, however, *in full view of the baby,* place the trinket under the pillow so it cannot be seen.

If you begin when your child is young enough, what you will discover is "out of sight, out of mind." The baby acts as though the trinket no longer exists and all reaching for it ceases. It appears as though infants at this age do not have object permanence, at least in this context.

Repeat the experiment every week or so and observe your baby's reaction. Sometime shortly after the baby is seven months old, you will observe a change. Your infant will show object permanence by reaching under the pillow to retrieve the trinket. Mom and Dad are so proud!

But the experiment is not quite finished. Once your child can retrieve the trinket from under the pillow, repeat the procedure, but put *two* pillows between you and your baby. Do everything as before but, after putting the trinket under the first pillow, take it out again (in full view of the baby) and place it under the second pillow. Once again you have stumped the child. He or she will reach under the first pillow, but then the game is over. Not finding the trinket under the first pillow, the baby is unable to track it to the second pillow, and so it is "out of sight, out of mind."

Continue by repeating this second procedure every few days. Within a short time your baby will master the problem and go directly to the second pillow. Object permanence in this context is now well established.

"Fearfully and Wonderfully Made"

God's hidden world of mystery and mechanism gives us freedom from concern over the fundamental requirements of our existence so that we might enjoy a higher life of love, wisdom, and creativity. There is in these discovered psychological mechanisms a witness to both the structure and stability provided for us by God through his creation and the rest and deliverance he provides for us through his salvation. Conditioning mechanisms help us to adjust automatically to changes in our environments, and without them life would be an unimaginable burden. Constancies operate effortlessly and unconsciously to give coherence, continuity, and stability to our experience, and without them life would be a bewildering jumble. Such mechanisms provide meaning and rest in our existence. They speak of God's gracious provision for our lives. They also testify to our dependence on God and his creation. We need God!

9

We Need God

His divine power has given us everything we need for life and godliness through our knowledge of him [Jesus Christ] who called us by his own glory and goodness (2 Peter 1:3 NIV).

God and his Word rescued me from a pit of intellectual despair into which I fell as a consequence of my studies in psychology. After I became a Christian, I re-examined my discipline from a biblical perspective. I came to realize, after discovering the writings of Henry Morris and other creation scientists, that biblical teaching about origins was scientifically superior to the evolutionist framework and was also the essential, foundational doctrine for understanding psychology and other academic disciplines.[1] "In the beginning God" and "man created in the image and likeness of God" were the pivotal truths that allowed me to escape my doubt about the meaningfulness of human existence (chapters 1 and 4). Biblical teaching about the Fall and the resultant weak and sinful nature of man (chapters 2 and 3) was the other vital doctrine that helped me bring the field into focus. Once I learned to keep these doctrines in mind, the research findings of psychology—as opposed to the speculation and armchair theorizing of many psychologists—served to strengthen and bless me in my faith rather than weaken it. I discovered that the hard evidence of psychology confirmed rather than contradicted Scripture. As stated at the outset, the purpose of this book has been to share with my readers the findings and insights from psychology that have blessed me, in hope that they too would be strengthened in their faith and drawn closer to God. To that end we proceeded to explore the field of psychology in the context of our biblical framework.

Man is created in the image of the Creator God and therefore takes joy in creativity and discovery about the world God has made (chapter 5). To be properly creative

84

and to understand correctly the discoveries God allows us to search out, we must remain faithful to his Word and commandments (chapter 6). As we do so, we uncover mysteries that cause us to glory in the wonder of God's creation. Scientific work becomes not only productive and a blessing to man, but a form of worship as well. In psychology we find abundant reasons to heighten our appreciation of God's gracious and loving provision for our lives (chapters 7 and 8). Now, in this final chapter, we turn one more time to what I believe is the deepest message of all.

Why We Need God Always

In the Garden of Eden, the serpent's temptation was that we could separate ourselves from God and be gods in our own right. The Bible refutes this lie, and scientific evidence from psychology echoes the message. The facts are clear: *We need God moment by moment.* We cannot stand on our own. The reason is obvious, considering (among other things) our knowledge of the conditioning mechanisms and constancies studied in the last chapter. Since we cannot constantly control and allow for the effects of these mechanisms, we are subject to all kinds of influences beyond our control. Psychologists have documented how subtle features of our surroundings shape our attitudes and actions in myriads of ways. These effects are usually not large, especially when they touch upon issues that are important to us. But, however slight, the existence of these influences shows that we cannot be our own gods in the manner of the serpent's temptation in the Garden of Eden.

For the believer who has repented of sin and returned to moment-by-moment fellowship with God through faith in the blood of the new covenant (Heb. 8), these mechanisms point to our rest and peace in dependence on Christ. We are "fearfully and wonderfully made," as the psalmist says. Regarding my eternal destiny and hope of everlasting life, my trust is in Christ, my creator, and now "the author and finisher" of my faith (Heb. 12:2). The many promises of God's provision are opened to me: "I will instruct thee and teach thee in the way which thou shalt go: I will guide thee with mine eye" (Ps. 32:8). "Only in the LORD are righteousness and strength" (Isa. 45:24a NASB). "God is my strength and power; And He makes my way perfect" (2 Sam. 22:33 NKJV). "And the Lord shall deliver me from every evil work, and will preserve me unto his heavenly kingdom" (2 Tim. 4:18). Because of this faith, I rejoice in the discovery of these psychological mechanisms that serve as reminders of God's faithful provision and my dependence upon him always.

For the unbeliever, on the other hand, these mechanisms speak to the eternal truth that we cannot be gods ourselves. They are a witness that we cannot fully determine our own actions and destiny in the manner of gods. We are part of a world that we have not created, and no matter how much we think we have gained control over it, the evidence from psychology shows that even in our innermost parts we are linked to and dependent on the rest of God's creation.

Finally, the scientific evidence from psychology points back to the fundamental spiritual issue facing each person: Whom will you serve? Will you strive to "be your own god" or will you cry out to the one who is truly God? The Bible is full of hope and promise for anyone who genuinely seeks to know and obey God. In the last chapter of the last book of the Bible, Jesus spoke in a vision to the apostle John and said, "Whoever is thirsty, let him come; and whoever wishes, let him take the free gift of the water of life" (Rev. 22:17b NIV).

God's offer is still open.

Appendix
Discussion Questions

Preface

1. How should a Christian use scientific evidence in Christian apologetics? Can scientific evidences ever be used legitimately? If so, what biblical and logical guidelines might you suggest for their use? What spiritual dangers are entailed in relying too much on scientific facts as a support of biblical faith? What spiritual dangers might result from a total dismissal of "facts that support the faith?" Give some biblical examples where facts and evidence were critical to faith.

2. This book uses three biblical doctrines to organize and interpret the data of psychology. Why do you feel each of these doctrines is or is not appropriate for understanding psychology? What other doctrines might you use to understand psychology? *Hint:* What about John 1? Are there elements in John 1 that might go beyond those used in this book?

Chapter 1

1. In what sense might an atheist psychologist say "man does not exist"? How would coming to believe in

the God of the Bible make a difference in that view of man?

2. What does it mean to be a determinist? What causes the future? Is it the past? Do we entirely of ourselves cause the future? If so, what causes us? Why is it essential to understand that God, rather than simply "the past," controls the future? If God and not merely "the past" controls the future, what is it about God's character that would cause scientists to trust that the cause-and-effect relationships they discover in the laboratory would continue to work in the future?

3. The author speaks of the crucial role of scientific evidences for biblical creation and against evolution in his understanding of psychology. What would be the implications for the nature of man if evolution were true? What would be the role of psychology if evolution were true? Since the Bible is true, why should we do research in psychology and study psychology? For example, what connection does studying psychology have with the Genesis mandate to subdue the earth? With the Great Commission? With loving your neighbor?

Chapter 2

1. Give some examples of rich and successful people who seemed to have had it all and yet turned out to be very unhappy. What can we learn from the example of their lives? What is it about your Christian faith that gives you peace and happiness in this life?

2. Give examples of "adaptation level" and "relative deprivation" from your own experience. What wisdom can we learn from these psychological concepts about peace and contentment in life? Can you name something bad that might happen to you in this life that could be made less fearful by understanding the adaptation-level concept? How might understanding these concepts be

helpful in enabling you to persevere, be patient in times of trouble, and be faithful through life to your present or future spouse and children?

3. Read and discuss Romans 7:14–25 in the context of Romans 6:1–8:17. From the standpoint of a counseling psychologist, how might this Scripture passage be good news and helpful in a counseling situation? What, if anything, about Romans 7:14–25 do you find comforting?

4. Discuss the two studies used to illustrate the fallen and sinful nature of man. Do you believe that psychologists should conduct this type of research? Is research necessary for a biblically based psychology? What kind of research should be conducted by a Bible-believing psychologist?

Chapter 3

1. The author argues that man needs God moment by moment. Give examples of ways we need God moment by moment. What would it mean if we were to say that we need God only once in a while? What are things we do that some might suppose we can do on our own, without God? Show how God would be needed in these situations after all.

2. Discuss social facilitation. What personal experiences can you think of where your own behavior might be influenced by a real or imagined audience? Describe a situation where social facilitation might help you to do the right thing. Describe a situation where social facilitation might influence you to sin.

3. One implication of the Hartshorne and May research on character in children is that people tend to have areas of strength and areas of weakness in their moral character. Consider Abraham, David, Peter, and

Paul. Identify areas of moral strength and weakness in their lives.

4. Discuss each of the five research examples presented as affording evidence of the sinful and weak nature of man's moral character. For each study, imagine what Jesus might do if God sent him to be a subject in the experiment. Would he even cooperate with the researchers? Under what conditions and for what purposes should people be willing to cooperate with psychology research?

5. What are some situations where you put the needs of someone else above your own, in obedience to 1 Corinthians 10:24 and 13:5?

6. Explain the four ways presented by the author to help Christians do right in the face of powerful and subtle temptations to evil all around us. Give an example of how each of these has been helpful in your own moral life.

Chapter 4

1. If you hold a pencil in the air and let go, it will drop to the floor. Scientists have discovered that the pencil always drops at the same exact speed. Unbelievers say it does so because of a natural law called gravity. How should a believer explain the phenomenon?

2. What causes the future? Unbelievers would say either that the past causes the future or, perhaps, that people cause the future. If people cause the future, what causes us? Most psychologists believe that the past causes people to be what they are, and, therefore, it comes back to the first option that the past causes the future. However, the Bible teaches that God knows and has control over the future. Discuss the differences

between "the past" and God as being in control of man's destiny. What would be the implications of these two alternatives for man's having a measure of control and choice regarding the future?

3. Discuss Stuart Cook's program to reduce racial prejudice. Do you believe research and "social engineering" efforts of this kind have a valid relationship to the Genesis 1:28 mandate to "fill the earth and subdue it"? What would be the place and limitations on social research and engineering in a biblically oriented culture?

4. Discuss the program for improving the mental health and outlook of elderly nursing-home residents. What is the crucial factor in making the approach work? What risks to the physical well-being of elderly persons might society be forced to accept in implementing such an approach?

5. Explain an atheist argument against the concept of human free-will and "meaningful self." Give a biblically based rebuttal to the atheist position and a defense of human moral choice and responsibility. Why do we need God?

Chapter 5

1. Why is belief in creativity in humans linked to belief in the God who is the creator of all things? What are two alternative approaches to dealing with human creativity for psychologists who deny God as creator?

2. T. G. R. Bower tried to establish a communication link with babies so that they could "answer his questions" about how they understood the world. Discuss the "answer" Bower got from his research. What is the significance of this answer?

3. Discuss the research studies indicating creativity and joy of discovery as basic to human nature. What is the biblical basis for human creativity and joy in discovery? Cite Scriptures.

Chapter 6

1. What are the two broad categories of influence that psychologists consider in trying to understand human development? Give examples of how God's grace and providence could work through each dimension. Give examples of how the effects of sin, the curse, and the fall could impact an individual life through each dimension.

2. Discuss a biblical perspective on microevolution, macroevolution, and the general theory of evolution.

Chapter 7

1. Give some examples from everyday speech that illustrate how human ingenuity and creativity allow language to expand to allow communication about new technologies and discoveries. On what basis would you argue that the creation of new terms and concepts does not offer evidence for evolution as providing an adequate explanation for the origin of language?

2. Give examples of important and fulfilling jobs that mentally handicapped people might be better suited to than their normally intelligent counterparts. What biblical concepts and principles might you draw on to encourage a better social treatment of mentally handicapped persons?

3. In what ways is the concept of "contingency-design" biblical?

Chapter 8

1. Discuss the example of the students who conditioned the author to lecture from one side of the room instead of the other. Under what conditions might it be morally justified and biblically proper to "condition" another person's behavior by controlling your responses to his/her actions?

2. How do conditioned behaviors help us in our everyday life? Give some examples. How would the experience of driving an automobile be different if God had not provided us with the conditioning mechanism?

3. Based on principles of conditioning, why should you obey traffic signals even when no traffic is in sight?

4. Try to imagine what life would be like without "object permanence." On the basis of this concept, why might babies enjoy peek-a-boo games more than adults?

5. How has reading this book changed your view of psychology?

Chapter 9

1. A popular song proclaims, "I did it my way." Do you think it is possible to escape the effects of others around us? Support your position with examples from the book.

2. What is the difference between "needing God" and "needing God moment by moment"? How would one's view of which represented the reality of our existence have a practical influence on his or her life?

3. What do you feel are the practical and positive implications of this book for your life?

Endnotes

Preface

1. Scripture attests to the important role of earthly evidences in witnessing to the truth of God's Word. Psalm 14:1 says that it is the fool who says in his heart that there is no God. One of the most significant passages is 2 Peter 3:3–7, where we are told that in the "last days" there will be "scoffers" who will be "willingly ignorant" of creation by the word of God and the worldwide, cataclysmic flood of Noah. Another arresting passage is John 3:12, where Jesus says to Nicodemus, "If I have told you earthly things, and ye believe not, how shall ye believe, if I tell you of heavenly things?" Both of these passages imply that "earthly" evidences witness to the validity of God's heavenly truth.

Chapter 1

1. B. F. Skinner, "A Lecture on 'Having' a Poem," *Cumulative Record: A Selection of Papers*, 3rd ed. (New York: Appleton-Century-Crofts, 1972), pp. 345–55.

2. Ibid., p. 354.

3. Ibid., pp. 354–55.

4. Henry Morris, *The Remarkable Birth of Planet Earth* (San Diego, Calif.: Creation-Life Pub., 1973).

5. Paul D. Ackerman, *It's A Young World After All* (Grand Rapids, Mich.: Baker Book House, 1986), p. 14.

Chapter 2

1. P. Brickman, D. Coates, and R. Janoff-Bulman, "Lottery Winners and Accident Victims: Is Happiness Relative?" *Journal of Personality and Social Psychology* 36, No. 8 (1978): 917–27.

2. G. A. Marlatt and B. E. Kaplan, "Self-initiated Attempts to Change Behavior: A Study of New Year's Resolutions," *Psychological Reports* 30 (1972): 123–31.

3. Paul goes on to point out that the answer is to be found only in Jesus Christ. One of the most blessed promises of Scripture follows this passage: "there is now no condemnation for those who are in Christ Jesus, because through Christ Jesus the law of the Spirit of life set me free from the law of sin and death" (Rom. 8:1–2 NIV).

4. D. L. McMillen and J. B. Austin, "Effect of Positive Feedback on Compliance Following Transgression," *Psychonomic Science* 24 (1971): 59-61.

5. The experiment and other aspects of its results were quite complicated. For example, the volunteer subjects who received illicit information apparently felt guilty about lying and were willing to compensate for their deceit. When asked to volunteer some time to help the experimenters, subjects in a condition where they had *not* received prior information about the study and thus had not lied volunteered an average of less than two minutes of time. The guilty subjects, however, volunteered an average of sixty-three minutes.

Other conditions of the experiment, however, greatly influenced subjects' reaction to having lied. For instance, when they were given feedback that they had done very well on the test, thus enhancing their course grade, those subjects *not* receiving illicit prior information and thus having not lied volunteered an average of forty minutes of time, while those receiving the prior information and subsequently lying to the experimenter volunteered an average of only eighteen minutes. The experimenters concluded that the most likely factor governing the subjects' response in the situation was protection of self-esteem rather than concern for right and wrong.

6. Stanley Milgram, "Behavioral Study of Obedience," *Journal of Abnormal and Social Psychology* 67 (1963): 371-78. For a complete report of Milgram's research program in destructive obedience see his book *Obedience to Authority* (New York: Harper & Row, 1974).

7. It was all an elaborate hoax. The impressive-looking machinery made noises but did not shock the victim. Furthermore, the "victim" was not a bona fide subject but a confederate in the experiment.

Chapter 3

1. N. Triplett, "The Dynamogenic Factors in Pacemaking and Competition," *American Journal of Psychology* 9 (1897): 507–33.

2. H. Hartshorne and M. A. May, *Studies in the Nature of Character* (Vol. 1). *Studies in Deceit* (New York: Macmillan, 1928).

3. Ibid., pp. 410–11.

4. Ibid., pp. 411–12. Emphasis added.

5. Psychologists call this human characteristic the "fundamental attribution error."

6. G. L. Wells and R. E. Petty, "The Effects of Overt Head Movements on Persuasion: Compatibility and Incompatibility of Responses," *Basic and Applied Social Psychology* 1 (1980): 219–30.

7. E. F. Loftus and J. C. Palmer, "Reconstruction of Automobile Destruc-

tion: An Example of the Interaction Between Language and Memory," *Journal of Verbal Learning and Verbal Behavior* 13 (1973): 585–89.

8. L. Berkowitz and A. LePage, "Weapons as Aggression-Eliciting Stimuli," *Journal of Personality and Social Psychology* 7 (1967): 202–7.

9. A. M. Isen and P. F. Levin, "Effect of Feeling Good on Helping: Cookies and Kindness," *Journal of Personality and Social Psychology* 21 (1972): 384–88. I have replicated this study with my own research students.

10. M. T. Orne, "On the Social Psychology of the Psychological Experiment: With Particular Reference to Demand Characteristics and Their Implications," *American Psychologist* 17 (1962): 776–83.

11. Ibid., pp. 777–78.

12. In casual conversation the self-serving bias is often masked by humility norms. Thus, a person may get an "A" on an exam and say, "I was just lucky." To unmask the humility norm and reveal the bias, all that is usually necessary is to agree with the person's attribution of his or her success to mere luck.

13. D. G. Myers, *Social Psychology* (New York: McGraw-Hill, 1983), p. 85.

14. Deuteronomy 6:6–7; Proverbs 19:18; 22:15; 29:15, 17; Ephesians 6:4.

15. My speciality is social psychology, the area within the field from which the research reported in this chapter was drawn. Much of it is humorous and fascinating, a bit like watching the "Candid Camera" television program. It is sometimes fun and appropriate to laugh at human foibles. However, when one stops to think about the deeper implications of the research in human character and human nature, as one must do in a college classroom, the result can be devastating to students' fragile optimism and sense of human dignity. As a result, several years ago I stopped teaching the social-psychology course. The problem is that there is too much potential for emotional and character damage when this subject matter is taught in the atmosphere of a state university, where there is not freedom to discuss and act on its full spiritual implications. I would want to teach social psychology only in a setting where the students were open to the Christian gospel, where I could incorporate the material within a context of Bible study, and where we were free to stop and pray in accordance with the spiritual implications of the material being studied.

Chapter 4

1. In this chapter I address what was for me the chief spiritual threat posed by the type of research findings presented in the previous chapter. Such findings led me to the "non-existence" discussed in chapter 1. I found the biblically based solution I present at the end of this chapter only *after* I became a Christian. The realization of the solution—found in the person of Christ himself—delivered me from tragic despair. It is a vital part of the armor of faith for any Christian student of psychology.

2. L. S. Wrightsman, *Social Psychology*, 2nd ed. (Monterey, Calif.: Brooks/Cole, 1977), pp. 83–84.

3. Ibid., p. 84.

4. Sigmund Freud, quoted in K. E. Scheibe, "The Psychologist's Advantage and Its Nullification," *American Psychologist* 33, No. 10 (October 1978): 874.

5. B. F. Skinner, quoted in W. T. Powers, "Quantitative Analysis of Purposive Systems: Some Spadework at the Foundations of Sc`entific Psychology," *Psychological Review* 85, No. 5 (1978): 417.

6. C. B. Bakker, "Why People Don't Change," *Psychotherapy: Theory, Research and Practice* 12, No. 2 (Summer 1975): 169.

7. R. V. Burton, "Generality of Honesty Reconsidered," *Psychological Review* 70, No. 6 (1963): 481–99; and E. A. Nelson, R. E. Grinder, and M. L. Mutterer, "Sources of Variance in Behavioral Measures of Honesty in Temptation Situations: Methodological Analyses," *Developmental Psychology* 1, No. 3 (1969): 265–79.

8. Wrightsman, *Social Psychology*, pp. 397–408.

9. Ibid., pp. 407–8.

10. The opposite error to the denial of free will and meaningful self is the contemporary "self-esteem movement." From a biblical point of view, elevating self is a much more common human tendency than denying the self's existence. Either extreme is unbiblical and flies in the face of genuine scientific evidence. Two excellent books pointing out the errors, spiritual deception, and danger of the self-esteem movement are William Kirk Kilpatrick's *Psychological Seduction: The Failure of Modern Psychology* (Nashville, Tenn.: Thomas Nelson, 1983), and Paul C. Vitz's *Psychology As Religion: The Cult of Self-Worship*, (Grand Rapids, Mich.: William B. Eerdmans, 1977).

11. E. J. Langer and J. Rodin, "The Effects of Choice and Enhanced Personal Responsibility for the Aged: A Field Experiment in an Institutional Setting," *Journal of Personality and Social Psychology* 34 (1976): 191–98.

12. In the context of discussion among believers, the free-will debate centers on consideration of Scripture passages relating to human choice and responsibility, in contrast to passages relating to God's sovereignty and predestination of saved souls. It is not within the scope of this book to cover the theological dimension of the free-will issue. I am arguing that the personal God of the Bible is the logical foundation for the *category* of free will. Any free choice made is by the grace of God and cannot limit the sovereignty of God.

Chapter 5

1. B. F. Skinner, *Cumulative Record: A Selection of Papers*, 3rd ed. (New York: Appleton-Century-Crofts, 1972), p. 354.

2. Abraham H. Maslow, "Creativity in Self-Actualizing People," in A. Rothenberg & C. R. Hausman, ed., *The Creativity Question* (Durham, N.C.: Duke University Press, 1976), p. 92.

3. T. G. R. Bower, "The Visual World of Infants," *Scientific American* 215 (1965): 80–92.

4. I believe that the dominion resulting from biblically obedient scientific research and discovery is one of the ways that Christians today fulfill the Lord's promise in John 14:12 that his disciples would do even greater works than his.

5. Material in this section is taken from T. G. R. Bower, *A Primer of Infant Development* (San Francisco: W. H. Freeman, 1977), pp. 42–45.

6. Ibid., pp. 43–44. The research in question was conducted by a Czech psychologist named H. Papousek. Details of Papousek's work may be found in H. Papousek, "Individual Variability in Learned Responses in Human Infants" in R. J. Robinson, ed., *Brain and Early Behaviour* (London: Academic Press, 1969).

7. Ibid., pp. 42–43.

Chapter 6

1. Michael Denton, *Evolution: A Theory in Crisis* (Bethesda, Md.: Adler & Adler, 1986), pp. 328–29.

2. Material in this section is drawn from an article published by the author several years ago: "Considerations Regarding a Creation Model for Experimental Psychology," *Creation Social Science and Humanities Quarterly* 1 (Spring 1979): 5–10.

3. Evolutionists have noted the phenomenon of over-design, although, of course, they do not refer to it in this way. The evolutionist term for this phenomenon is "surplusage," which psychologists have noted most particularly as the excess of learning capacity beyond what is useful for survival. Specifically, research animals exhibit learning capabilities in laboratory experiments that are neither apparent nor relevant to survival in their natural habitats. For discussion see Robert Boice, "Surplusage," *Bulletin of the Psychonomic Society* 9 (1977): 452–54.

4. T. G. R. Bower, "The Visual World of Infants," *Scientific American* 215 (1965): 80–92.

5. See Roger Lewin, "Evolutionary Theory Under Fire," *Science* 210 (November 21, 1980): 883–87.

Chapter 7

1. The same contingency-design combination is apparent to some degree in all intelligent animals. However, the learning and adaptability of animals is miniscule compared to humans. Therefore, the capacity for back-up of faulty or environmentally inappropriate instinctual systems is highly limited.

2. G. P. Sackett, "Monkeys Reared in Isolation with Pictures as Visual Input: Evidence for an Innate Releasing Mechanism," *Science* 154 (1966): 1468–73.

3. A. N. Meltzoff and M. K. Moore, "Imitation of Facial and Manual Gestures by Human Neonates," *Science* 198 (1977): 75–78.

4. Laura E. Berk, *Child Development* (Boston: Allyn and Bacon, 1989), p. 152.

5. Ibid., p. 375.

6. N. Chomsky, "Language and the Mind," *Readings in Educational Psychology Today* (Del Mar, Calif.: CRM Books, 1970), p. 152.

7. Ibid., p. 155.

8. Ibid.

9. This is Louis S. B. Leakey's view as expressed in dialogue with Robert Ardrey, printed in *Psychology Today*, September 1972, p. 73ff. See especially pp. 75–76.

10. Henry M. Morris, "Language, Creation and the Inner Man," *The Battle*

for Creation: Acts/Facts/Impacts Volume 2, ed. by Henry M. Morris & Duane Gish (Creation Life Publishers [now Master Books], P.O. Box 1606, El Cajon, CA 92022), pp. 286–98.

11. G. G. Simpson, "The Biological Nature of Man," *Science* 152 (April 22, 1966), p. 477 (cited in Morris, p. 292).

12. Albert C. Baugh, *A History of the English Language* (New York: Appleton-Century-Crofts, 1957) p. 10. (Emphasis added.) Cited in Morris, p. 293.

13. "Half a Brain: Youth With Drastic Surgery Ends Up Smarter Than Most," *The Wichita Eagle-Beacon*, November 8, 1976, p. 1Aff.

14. Ibid., p. 1.

15. Ibid., p. 6A.

16. R. Lewin, "Is Your Brain Really Necessary?" *Science* 210 (December 12, 1980): 1232–34.

17. Ibid., p. 1232.

18. Ibid.

19. Ibid.

20. Ibid., p. 1234.

21. N. Hunt, *The World of Nigel Hunt* (New York: Garrett, 1967).

22. H. M. Skeels, "Adult Status of Children with Contrasting Early Life Experiences: A Follow-up Study," *Monographs of the Society for Research in Child Development* 31, Serial No. 105 (1966).

Chapter 8

1. Conditioning is a largely unconscious and automatic process, whereby psychological behavior reflects regularities and adjusts to changes in environmental contingencies.

2. An application of this knowledge for education is obvious. In driver-education programs, the discoveries psychologists have made regarding conditioning mechanisms give us good material for explaining to student drivers important personal reasons for obeying traffic regulations. People are much more obedient to and respectful of regulations when they know good, personally relevant reasons that underlie them.

3. F. W. Snyder and N. H. Pronko, *Vision With Spatial Inversion* (Wichita, Kans.: University of Wichita Press, 1952), pp. 142–43.

4. A. N. Meltzoff and M. K. Moore, "Imitation of Facial and Manual Gestures by Human Neonates," *Science* 198 (1977): 75–78.

5. T. G. R. Bower, "Repetitive Processes in Child Development" in *Mind and Behavior: Readings From Scientific American* (San Francisco: W. H. Freeman, 1980), pp. 64–73. Bower has discussed this fascinating phenomenon at length, giving many examples of abilities that appear early in "seed" form, only to go underground until through a proper combination of maturation and exercise they appear in their manifest form. For example, Bower reports that the infant's ability to imitate facial expressions in the first weeks after birth "soon seems to fade away, reappearing only toward the end of the child's first year" (p. 64). Equally remarkable, "infants can reach out to

touch visible objects and will occasionally even grasp them. That eye-hand coordination also disappears at the age of about four weeks and will not be seen again until the age of some 20 weeks" (p. 64).

Chapter 9

1. In 1977 I helped found the Creation Social Science and Humanities Society for the purpose of promoting and disseminating information on the implications of biblical creation for social sciences and humanities. In 1978 we began publishing the *Creation Social Science and Humanities Quarterly*. This book is an outgrowth of that work. (Interested persons may contact CSSHS at 1429 N. Holyoke, Wichita, KS 67208.)